Management
on the
World Wide Web

Management
on the
World Wide Web

Cynthia B. Leshin

 Prentice Hall, Upper Saddle River, New Jersey 07458

Acquisitions Editor:	Natalie Anderson
Associate Editor:	Lisamarie Brassini
Editorial Assistant:	Chrissy Statuto
Editor-in-Chief:	James Boyd
Marketing Manager:	Sandra Steiner
Production Editor:	Maureen Wilson
Production Coordinator:	Renee Pelletier
Managing Editor:	Carol Burgett
Manufacturing Buyer:	Kenneth J. Clinton
Manufacturing Supervisor:	Arnold Vila
Manufacturing Manager:	Vincent Scelta
Design Director:	Patricia Wosczyk

Netscape Communications Corporation™ Copyright

Netscape Communications Corporation (NCC), Netscape, Netscape Navigator, and Netsite are trademarks or registered trademarks of Netscape Communications Corporation. Netscape Communications Corporation has granted permission to use screen captures from their home page and to describe Netscape Navigator and its interface. Whereas Netscape's tutorial has been referred to, all efforts have been made not to copy this document.

Prentice-Hall International (UK) Limited, *London*
Prentice-Hall of Australia Pty. Limited, *Sydney*
Prentice-Hall Canada Inc., *Toronto*
Prentice-Hall Hispanoamericana, S. A., *Mexico*
Prentice-Hall of India Private Limited, *New Delhi*
Prentice-Hall of Japan, Inc., *Tokyo*
Simon & Schuster Asia Pte. Ltd., *Singapore*
Editora Prentice-Hall do Brasil, Ltda., *Rio de Janeiro*

Printed in the United States of America
10 9 8 7 6 5 4 3 2 1

ISBN: 0-13-268871-9

DISCLAIMER

While a great deal of care has been taken to provide accurate and current information, the Internet is a dynamic and rapidly changing environment. Information may be in one place today and either gone or in a new location tomorrow. New sites come up daily; others disappear. Some sites provide forwarding address information; others do not. The publisher and author assume no responsibility for errors or omissions. Neither is any liability assumed for damages resulting from the use of this information.

As you travel the information superhighway and find that a resource you are looking for can no longer be found at a given Internet address, there are several steps you can take:

1. Check for a new Internet address or link, often provided on the site of the old address.

2. Use one of the search engines described in Chapter 5 with the title of the Internet resource as keywords.

3. Explore Internet databases such as Excite, Yahoo, Infoseek, or Galaxy which have large directories of Internet business resources.

The author welcomes readers' feedback, correction of inaccuracies, and suggestions for improvements in subsequent editions. Cynthia Leshin can be contacted by e-mail at: **cleshin@xplora.com**

NOTE: This guide presents Netscape Navigator 2.0. Subsequent updates (Navigator 2.02 and 3.0) have few noticeable changes for Internet navigation and communication. Navigator 2.02 has security enhancements. Navigator 3.0 added fully integrated audio, video, 3D, and Internet telephone communication capabilities. These capabilities make it possible to hear audio, watch movies, and travel through 3D worlds without adding separate helper application software.

About the Author

Cynthia Leshin is an educational technologies specialist with her doctorate in educational technology from Arizona State University. Dr. Leshin has her own publishing, training, and consulting company. She has authored six books: *Internet Adventures — Step-by-Step Guide to Finding and Using Educational Resources*, *Netscape Adventures — Step-by-Step Guide to Netscape Navigator and the World Wide Web*, *Internet Investigations in Electronics*, *Internet Investigations in Criminal Justice*, *Internet Investigations in Business Communication*, and *Instructional Design: Strategies and Tactics*. The last of these is being used in graduate programs. Her company, XPLORA, publishes the *Internet Adventures* quarterly newsletter to assist teachers with integrating the Internet into the curriculum. Additionally, she is currently writing discipline specific Internet books and Internet-based learning activities for Prentice Hall.

Dr. Leshin has taught computer literacy and Internet classes at Arizona State University West and Estrella Mountain Community College. She currently teaches Internet classes using distance learning technology for Educational Management Group, a Simon & Schuster company. The Internet serves as a tool for teaching and communicating with her students. Her World Wide Web site is a learning resource for students and is also used when making presentations.

Dr. Leshin consults with schools and businesses interested in connecting to the Internet. Her expertise in educational psychology and theories of learning provides her with a unique background for translating complicated technical information into an easy-to-use, easy-to-understand, practical learning resource.

In Dr. Leshin's "other life" she rides mountain bikes and races for the Arizona Cannondale/Bud Lite race team. She also enjoys organic gardening, hiking, and exploring southwestern trails with her three dogs and husband, Steve.

CONTENTS

PART II — The Web and Management

Preface......................................

Management on the World Wide Web meets the needs of professors, students, and others interested in learning how to use the Internet as a powerful communication and information retrieval tool. This cutting edge guide provides step-by-step, easy-to-follow practical information to help you begin using the Internet for finding valuable information and for communicating within the global community.

Effective communication is key to the success of businesses worldwide. Customer and employee satisfaction are equally tangible elements to that success. Customers' perceived degree of responsiveness and the quality of communication from a company are central to building long-term relationships. Productive, efficient, and happy employees generally enjoy open communication channels between management and staff within their organizations. Therefore, continuing knowledge of current communication tools is essential in today's business world.

Methods of communication have changed dramatically over the past two decades. Before the 1970s, communication with customers and employees was either in person, by telephone, or by U.S. mail. In the 1980s, new communication tools began to emerge with the introduction of fax machines, personal computers, computer networks, electronic mail, express mail, cellular phones, and telecommunication technologies.

No one, not even corporate giants such as Microsoft, envisioned how the Internet would change our world. No one could have prophesied that the Internet of the 1970s and 1980s based at our educational institutions would become the fastest growing communication medium of all times. Today we are experiencing perhaps the greatest revolution in communication. Some have called the World Wide Web the fourth media, positioned to take a place with print, radio, and television as a mass market means of communication.

This new medium has changed the way we work, do business, communicate, access information, and spend our leisure time. The world is being transformed by the digital revolution, and those who do not join this webolution will be left behind. The Internet is not a trend. It is like an ever-cresting wave being driven by the force and momentum of international currents, spraying its global magic from the monitor and inviting us to jump in—the world awaits. Travel, information-on-demand, and communication make the Internet a technology that is here to stay.

But we are still pioneers in exploring the uses of this powerful new tool. At home, at school, or at work, children and adults alike are fascinated with the entertainment and edification aspects of the Internet. Individuals and businesses—from Fortune 500 companies to small sole proprietorships—are establishing their links in cyberspace, browsing for new customers, new profits, a new way to do business, even a new way to live. Opportunities for commerce and the private sector to find good matches to their personal interests, in trade, and/or employment are quickly becoming unlimited.

Many companies, in fact, are turning to the Internet to find employees, believing that the people who keep up with the most current information and technology advances in their field will be the best candidates for employment. These professionals are already cybersurfing, networking with peers, researching information, asking questions, and learning collaboratively from others around the world.

And now *Management on the World Wide Web* provides the foundation you need to begin using the Internet to communicate and to access and disseminate information. In this book, you will learn about browsers, the software programs that make it possible to navigate the Internet and view multimedia resources (text, images, video, and sound) on the World Wide Web—simply by pointing and clicking your mouse.

In Chapter 4 (Chatting on the Net) you will learn about Internet communication tools— listserv mailing lists, Usenet newsgroups, Internet Relay Chat (IRC), Internet phones, and Internet videoconferencing.

In Chapter 5 you will learn how to use search tools to find valuable information and resources on the Internet. You will also learn how to do business research using search engines, directories, and Internet collections.

Chapter 6 introduces the earliest Internet tools and resources—Gopher, FTP (File Transfer Protocol), and Telnet. Although the Web is the center of Internet activity, there are many different and valuable non-Web resources.

Chapter 7 introduces you to many excellent business and management resources on the Internet. You will find many of the best Web sites in Management, Organizational Behavior, Entrepreneurship, Small Business, Global Business, and Human Resource Management. You will learn how the Internet opens new doors to a global community willing to share the latest information in management.

By exploring the resources in Chapter 7 you will begin to better understand the power of the Internet as a new tool for managers. Visit World Wide Web sites and analyze how they are promoting their company, communicating with customers, building relationships, sharing information, and perhaps most importantly, what the design elements are that attract customers and keep them returning. Learn how to acquire the latest information that will help you as a manager. This information is acquired through Internet sites and by communicating within the global community.

Chapter 8 provides activities to facilitate learning how to use the Internet as a valuable tool in management. It provides the foundation for understanding how the Internet is being used in management and how a management professional can use this powerful new medium for communication, information access, and information dissemination.

Chapters 9, 10, and 11 explore how to use the Internet for career planning and finding job opportunities in the business. You will learn how to showcase your talents and skills and improve your chances for getting a job by creating an electronic résumé. And, most importantly, you will learn how to use the Internet as a valuable and important tool for your personal and professional life.

The Appendices provide valuable information for connecting to the Internet and finding an Internet provider.

Your journey will be divided into two parts:

PART I: Understanding the Internet

PART II: The Web and Management

Happy Internet Adventures

Acknowledgments...

The author expresses special thanks to all who have helped develop this book.

I am most grateful to Natalie Anderson for the opportunity to write this book.

To my copy editors, Norma Nelson and Nancy Dupree for their most appreciated suggestions to improve my writing.

Special appreciation to James V. Dupree for his review and for the thoughtful and important recommendations in the management content.

To my son, Todd Haughton, for the business collage.

To Maureen Wilson, production editor, and all the other personnel at Prentice Hall who have transformed these words into this guide, especially those who read the manuscript and made valuable and most appreciated suggestions.

To my husband, Steve, for his continuing support and for helping to make this Internet adventure possible.

Management
on the
World Wide Web

PART I

Understanding the Internet

CHAPTER 1
What Is the Internet?

• •

In this chapter, you will learn

- ➤ what it means to "be on the Internet."
- ➤ the difference between the Internet and the World Wide Web.
- ➤ Internet addressing protocol—the URL.
- ➤ the three standards used by the World Wide Web.

• •

What Is the Internet?

in′ter•net n
1. world's largest information network **2.** global
web of computer networks **3.** inter-network of many
networks all running the TCP/IP protocol
4. powerful communication tool **5.** giant highway
system connecting computers and the regional
and local networks that connect these computers
syn **information superhighway, infobahn,
data highway, electronic highway, Net,
cyberspace**

The term most frequently used to refer to the Internet is "information superhighway." This superhighway is a vast network of computers connecting people and resources around the world. The Internet is accessible to anyone with a computer and a modem.

The Internet began in 1969 when a collection of computer networks was developed. The first network was sponsored by the United States Department of Defense in response to a need for military institutions and universities to share their research. In the 1970s, government and university networks continued to develop as many organizations and companies began to build private computer networks. In the late 1980s, the National Science Foundation (NSF) created five supercomputer centers at major universities. This special network is the foundation of the Internet today.

Computer networks were initially established to share information among institutions that were physically separate. Throughout the years these networks have grown and the volume and type of information made available to people outside these institutions have also continued to evolve and grow. Today we can exchange electronic mail, conduct research, and look at and obtain files that contain text information, graphics, sound, and video. As more and more schools, universities, organizations, and institutions develop new resources, they are made available to us through our computer networks. These networks make it possible for us to be globally interconnected with each other and to this wealth of information.

What Does It Mean To "Be on the Internet"?

"Being on the Internet" means having full access to all Internet services. Any commercial service or institution that has full Internet access provides the following:

- Electronic mail (e-mail)
- Telnet
- File Transfer Protocol (FTP)
- World Wide Web

Electronic Mail

Electronic mail is the most basic, the easiest to use, and for many people, the most useful Internet service. E-mail services allow you to send, forward, and receive messages from people all over the world, usually at no charge. You can then easily reply to, save, file, and categorize received messages.

Electronic mail also makes it possible to participate in electronic conferences and discussions. You can use e-mail to request information from individuals, universities, and institutions.

Telnet

Telnet provides the capability to login to a remote computer and to work interactively with it. When you run a Telnet session, your computer is remotely connected to a computer at another location, but will act as if it were directly connected to that computer.

File Transfer Protocol (FTP)

File Transfer Protocol is a method that allows you to move files and data from one computer to another. File Transfer Protocol, most commonly referred to as FTP, enables you to download magazines, books, documents, free software, music, graphics, and much more.

World Wide Web (WWW or Web)

The World Wide Web is a collection of standards and protocols used to access information available on the Internet. World Wide Web users can easily access text documents, images, video, and sound.

The Web and the Internet

The World Wide Web is a collection of documents linked together in what is called a *hypermedia system*. Links point to any location on the Internet that can contain information in the form of text, graphics, video, or sound files.

Using the World Wide Web requires "browsers" to view Web documents and navigate through the intricate link structure. Currently there are between 30-40 different Web browsers. In this guide you will learn how to use two of the premiere Web browsers—Netscape Navigator and Microsoft Internet Explorer. Both of these browsers combine a point-and-click interface design with an "open" architecture that is capable of integrating other Internet tools such as electronic mail, FTP, Gopher, and Usenet newsgroups. This architecture makes it relatively easy to incorporate images, video, and sound into text documents.

The World Wide Web was developed at the European Particle Physics Laboratory (CERN) in Geneva, Switzerland as a means for physicists to share papers and data easily. It has evolved into a sophisticated technology that can now link hypertext and hypermedia documents.

The Web and the Internet are *not* synonymous. The World Wide Web is a collection of standards and protocols used to access information available on the Internet. The Internet is the network used to transport information.

The Web uses three standards:

- URLs (Uniform Resource Locators)
- HTTP (Hypertext Transfer Protocol)
- HTML (Hypertext Markup Language)

These standards provide a mechanism for WWW servers and clients to locate and display information available through other protocols such as Gopher, FTP, and Telnet.

URLs (Uniform Resource Locators)

URLs are a standard format for identifying locations on the Internet. They also allow an addressing system for other Internet protocols such as access to Gopher menus, FTP file retrieval, and Usenet newsgroups. URLs specify three types of information needed to retrieve a document:

- the protocol to be used;
- the server address to which to connect; and
- the path to the information.

The format for a URL is: **protocol//server-name/path**

FIGURE 1.1
Sample URLs

World Wide Web URL: http://home.netscape.com/home/
                      welcome.html
Document from a secure
server: https://netscape.com
Gopher URL: gopher://umslvma.umsl.edu/Library
FTP URL: ftp://nic.umass.edu
Telnet URL: telnet://geophys.washington.edu
Usenet URL: news:rec.humor.funny

NOTE

The URL for newsgroups omits the two slashes. The two slashes designate the beginning of a server name. Since you are using your Internet provider's local news server, you do not need to designate a news server by adding the slashes.

URL TIPS...

▣ Do not capitalize the protocol string. For example, the HTTP protocol should be **http://** not **HTTP://**. Some browsers such as Netscape correct these errors; others do not.

▣ If you have trouble connecting to a Web site, check your URL to be sure you have typed the address correctly.

▣ Netscape 2.0 and 3.0 accept abbreviated Net addresses, without the **http://www prefix**. If you type a single word as your URL, Netscape adds the prefix **http://ww.** and the **suffix.com**. For example, to connect to Netscape's Home page, type **Netscape**. Explorer requires the **http://www.prefix.**

HTTP (Hypertext Transfer Protocol)

HTTP is a protocol used to transfer information within the World Wide Web. Web site URLs begin with the http protocol:

http://

This Web URL connects you to Netscape's Home Page.

http://home.netscape.com

HTML (Hypertext Markup Language)

HTML is the programming language used to create a Web page. It formats the text of the document, describes its structure, and specifies links to other documents. HTML also includes programming to access and display different media such as images, video, and sound.

The Adventure Begins...

Now that you have a basic understanding of the Internet, you are ready to begin your adventure. Before you can travel and explore the information superhighway, you will first need the following:

- an Internet account

- a username and password (required to log onto your Internet account)

- instructions from your institution on how to log on and log off

Getting Started

1. Turn on your computer.
2. Log onto your network using your institution's login procedures.
3. Open Netscape Navigator, Explorer, or the Internet browser that you will be using.

CHAPTER 2
Guided Tour—
Internet Browsers

• •

This chapter provides you with a guided tour of the two most widely used Internet browsers—Netscape Navigator and Microsoft Internet Explorer. You will learn

➠ how to navigate the Internet by using toolbar buttons and pull-down menus.
➠ how to save your favorite Internet sites (URLs) as bookmarks.

• •

Netscape Navigator

Netscape Navigator is a user-friendly graphical browser for the Internet. Netscape makes it possible to view and interact with multimedia resources (text, images, video, and sound) by pointing-and-clicking your mouse on pull-down menus and toolbar buttons.

Netscape Navigator (Version1.0) was developed in 1994 by Marc Andreessen and others who also developed the first graphical Internet browser, Mosaic, at the National Center for Supercomputing Applications (NCSA) at the University of Illinois at Champaign-Urbana. It quickly became the standard and was the premiere Internet information browser in 1995. Netscape Navigator 2.0 was introduced in February 1996; Navigator 3.0 was introduced in August 1996.

Features and Capabilities

Netscape Navigator features include the ability to

• use Netscape as your electronic mail program.

- connect to Gopher, FTP, and Telnet sites without using any additional software.
- read Usenet newsgroups.
- save your favorite Internet addresses (URLs) as bookmarks.
- download images, video, and sound files to your computer desktop.
- view, save, or print the HTML programming code for Web pages as either text or HTML source code.
- use plug-in programs, such as JAVA, RealAudio, and Shockwave that extend the capabilities of Netscape.

The Netscape Window (page)

The World Wide Web is unique in that its architecture allows multimedia resources to be incorporated into a hypertext file or document called a *page*. A Web page or *window* may contain text, images, movies, and sound. Each multimedia resource on a page has associated locational information to link you to the resource. This locational information is called the URL.

The Netscape Navigator window includes the following features to assist you with your Internet travels:

- The *Window Title Bar* shows the name of the current document.

- *Page display* shows the content of the Netscape window. A page includes text and links to images, video, and sound files. Links include highlighted words (colored and/or underlined) or icons. Click on a highlighted word or icon to bring another page of related information into view.

- *Frames* is a segmented portion of a Netscape page that contains its own page. See page 248 for more information on frames.

- *Progress Bar* shows the completed percentage of your document layout as your page downloads.

- *Mail Icon* (the small envelope in the bottom-right corner of the Netscape page, or the Mail and News pages) provides you with information on the status of your mail. A question mark next to the mail envelope indicates that Netscape cannot automatically check the mail server for new e-mail messages.

- *Address location* field shows the URL address of the current document.

- *Toolbar* buttons activate Netscape features and navigational aids.

- *Directory* buttons display resources for helping you to browse the Internet.

- Security indicators (*doorkey icon* in the lower-left corner of the window) identify whether a document is secure (doorkey icon is blue) or insecure (doorkey icon is grey).

The Home Page

The Home Page as shown in Figure 2.1 is the starting point for your journey using a Web browser such as Netscape Navigator. Home pages are created by Internet providers, colleges and universities, schools, businesses, individuals, or anyone who has information they want to make available on the Internet. For example, a college or university may have links to information on the college and courses taught.

FIGURE 2.1
A Home Page for Intel
http://www.intel.com

Navigating With Netscape

This guided tour introduces you to Netscape's graphical interface navigational tools:

- hyperlinks
- toolbar buttons
- pull-down menus

Hyperlinks

When you begin Netscape you will start with a Home Page. Click on highlighted words (colored and/or underlined) to bring another page of related information to your screen.

Images will automatically load onto this page unless you have turned off the **Auto Load Images** found under the **Options** menu. If you have turned off this option you will see this icon which represents an image that can be downloaded.

If you want to view this image, click on the highlighted icon or on the **Images** button.

As you travel the World Wide Web, you will find other icons to represent movies, video, and sound. Click on these icons to download (link) to these resources.

Toolbar Buttons

Netscape toolbar buttons

⇦○	○⇨	🏠	🔄	🖼	⇨○	🖨	🔍	○
Back	Forward	Home	Reload	Images	Open	Print	Find	Stop

■ **Back:** Point-and-click on the **Back** button to go to your previous page.

■ **Forward:** This button takes you to the next page of your history list. The history list keeps track of the pages you link to.

Home: This button takes you back to the first opening page that you started with.

Reload: Click on this button to reload the same page that you are viewing. Changes made in the source page will be shown in this new page.

Images: Clicking on this button downloads images onto your current page. Netscape provides you with an option to not download images when you access a page. This makes page downloading faster. If you have selected this option (found in **Options** menu—**Auto Load Images**) and decide that you would like to view an image, just click on the **Images** button.

Open: Use this button to access a dialog box for typing in URLs for Web sites, newsgroups, Gopher, FTP, and Telnet.

Print: Select this button to print the current page you are viewing.

Find: If you are searching for a word in the current page you are viewing, click on the **Find** button for a dialog box to enter the word or phrase.

Stop: This button stops the downloading of Web pages: text, images, video, or sound.

Netscape navigational buttons for exploring the Net

What's New?	What's Cool?	Handbook	Net Search	Net Directory	Software

What's New: Visit *What's New* to link to the best new sites.

What's Cool: Netscape's selection of cool Web sites to visit.

Handbook: Links you to online Netscape tutorials, references, and index.

■ **Net Search:** Clicking on this button links you to available search engines that help find a particular site or document. Search engines use keywords and concepts to help find information in titles or headers of documents, directories, or the entire documents.

■ **Net Directory:** Click on this button to explore Internet resources categorized by topic. Some directories cover the entire Internet; some present only what they feel is relevant; others focus on a particular field.

■ **Software:** This button connects you to information about Netscape Navigator software: subscription programs, upgrade information, and registration.

Pull-Down Menus

Nine pull-down menus offer navigational tools for your Netscape journeys: File, Edit, View, Go, Bookmarks, Options, Directory, Window, and Help (Windows only).

File Menu

Many of the **File** menu options work the same as they do in other applications. You also have options to open a new Netscape window, Home Page, or Internet site.

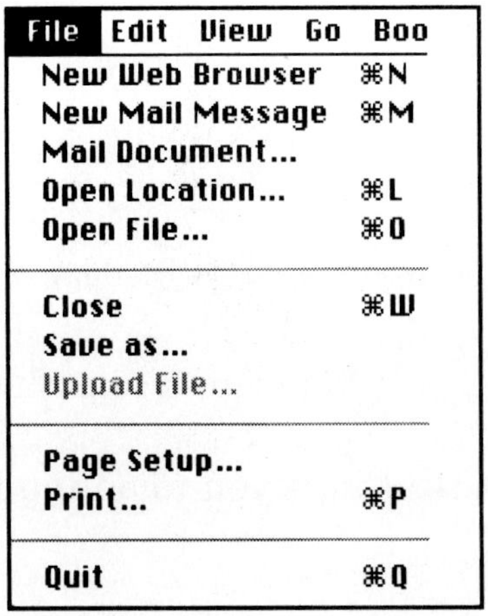

FIGURE 2.2

Netscape **File** pull-down menu

File	Edit	View	Go	Boo
New Web Browser				⌘N
New Mail Message				⌘M
Mail Document...				
Open Location...				⌘L
Open File...				⌘O
Close				⌘W
Save as...				
Upload File...				
Page Setup...				
Print...				⌘P
Quit				⌘Q

New Web Browser: Creates a new Netscape window. This window displays the first page you viewed when you connected to Netscape.

New Mail Message: Opens an e-mail composition box that allows you to create and send a message or attach a document to your mail message.

Mail Document (or Mail Frame): Lets you send an e-mail message with the Web page you are viewing attached. The page's URL will be included.

Open Location: Works the same as the **Open** toolbar button. Enter a URL address in the dialog box.

Open File: Provides a dialog box to open a file on your computer's hard drive. For example, you can open a Web image downloaded to your hard drive without being connected to the Internet.

Close: Closes the current Netscape page. On Windows, this option exits the Netscape application when you close the last page.

Save as... (or Save Frame as): Creates a file to save the contents of the current Internet page you are viewing in the Netscape window. The page can be saved as plain text or in source (HTML) format.

Upload File: Click on this option to upload a file to the FTP server indicated by the current URL. You can also upload images by dragging and dropping files from the desktop to the Netscape window. **NOTE:** This command is active only when you are connected to an FTP server.

Page Setup: Click on this to specify your printing options.

Print: Click on this button to print the current page or frame. To print a single frame, click in the desired frame.

Print Preview (Windows only): Previews the printed page on the screen.

Exit (on Macintosh—Quit): Exits the Netscape application.

Edit Menu

The **Edit** menu makes it possible to cut and paste text from a Web page to your computer's clipboard. This option can be used to copy and paste text from a page or frame to a word processing document or another application of your choice. The options under this menu are similar to what you have available in many of your computer software applications under their **File** menus (i.e., word processing, desktop publishing, and graphics applications).

FIGURE 2.3
Netscape **Edit** menu

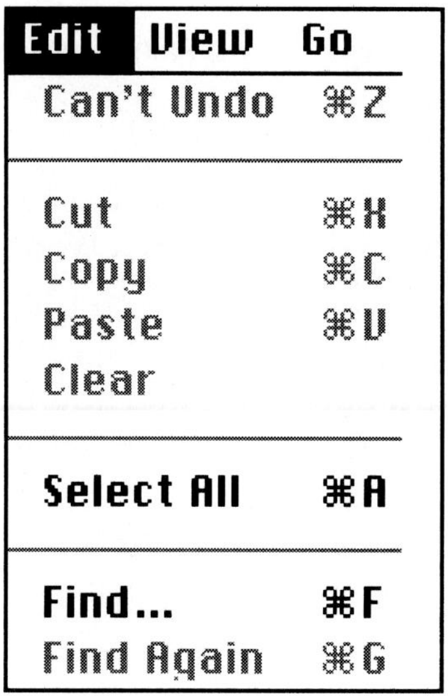

Edit	View	Go
Can't Undo		⌘Z
Cut		⌘X
Copy		⌘C
Paste		⌘V
Clear		
Select All		⌘A
Find...		⌘F
Find Again		⌘G

- **Undo...** (or **Can't Undo**): May reverse the last action you performed.

- **Cut:** Removes what you have selected and places it on the clipboard.

- **Copy:** Copies the current selection to the computer's clipboard.

- **Paste:** Puts the current clipboard's contents in the document you are working on.

- **Clear** (for the Macintosh only): Removes the current selection.

◨ **Select All:** Selects all you have indicated by using the application's selection markers. May be used to select items before you cut, copy, or paste.

◨ **Find:** Lets you search for a word or phrase within the current Web page.

◨ **Find Again:** Searches for another occurrence of the word or phrase specified when you used the **Find** command.

View Menu

The **View** menu offers options for viewing images, the Netscape page, HTML source code, and information on the current Web's document structure.

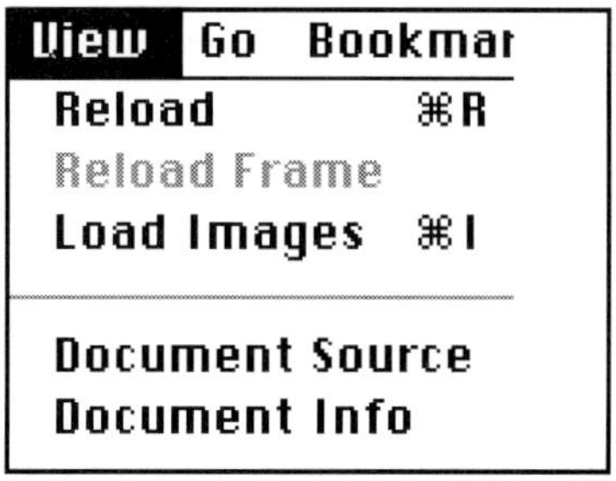

FIGURE 2.4
View menu options from Netscape

View	Go	Bookmar
Reload		⌘R
Reload Frame		
Load Images		⌘I
Document Source		
Document Info		

◨ **Reload:** Downloads a new copy of the current Netscape page you are viewing to replace the one originally loaded. Netscape checks the network server to see if any changes have occurred to the page.

◨ **Reload Frame:** Downloads a new copy of the currently selected page within a single frame on a Netscape page.

◨ **Load Images:** If you have set **Auto Load Images** in your Netscape **Options** menu, images from a Web page will be automatically loaded. If this option has not been selected, choose **Load Images** to display the current Netscape page.

◨ **Refresh** (Windows only): Downloads a new copy of the current Netscape page from local memory to replace the one originally loaded.

■ **Document Source:** Selecting this option provides you with the format of HTML (HyperText Markup Language). The HTML source text contains programming commands used to create the page.

■ **Document Info:** Produces a page in a separate Netscape window with information on the current Web document's structure and composition, including title, location (URL), date of the last modification, character set encoding, and security status.

Go Menu

The **Go** menu has Netscape navigational aids.

FIGURE 2.5
Netscape **Go** menu

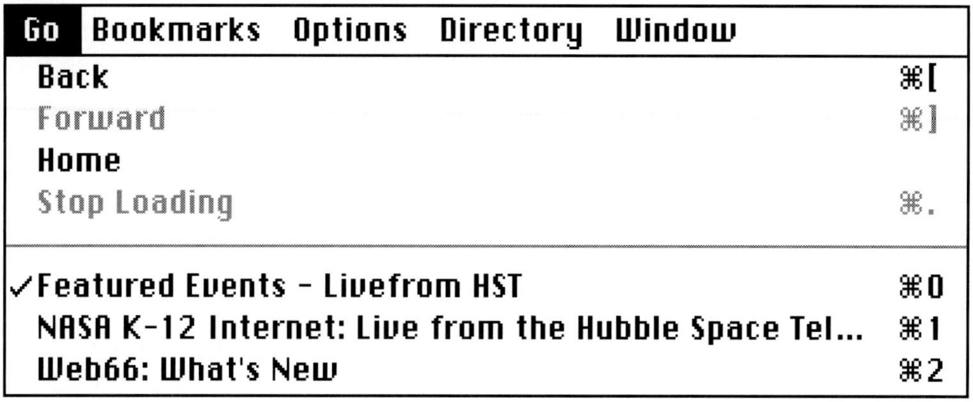

Go	Bookmarks	Options	Directory	Window	
Back					⌘[
Forward					⌘]
Home					
Stop Loading					⌘.
✓Featured Events - Livefrom HST					⌘0
NASA K-12 Internet: Live from the Hubble Space Tel...					⌘1
Web66: What's New					⌘2

■ **Back:** Takes you back to the previous page in your history list. Same as the **Back** button on the toolbar. The history list keeps track of all the pages you link to.

■ **Forward:** Takes you to the next page of your history list. Same as the **Forward** button on the toolbar.

■ **Home:** Takes you to the Home Page. Same as the **Home** button on the toolbar.

◙ **Stop Loading:** Stops downloading the current page. Same as the **Stop** button.

◙ **History Items:** A list of the titles of the places you have visited. Select menu items to display their pages. To view the History list, select the **Window** menu and then choose **History.**

Bookmarks Menu

Bookmarks makes it possible to save and organize your favorite Internet visits. Opening this pull-down menu allows you to view and download your favorite pages quickly.

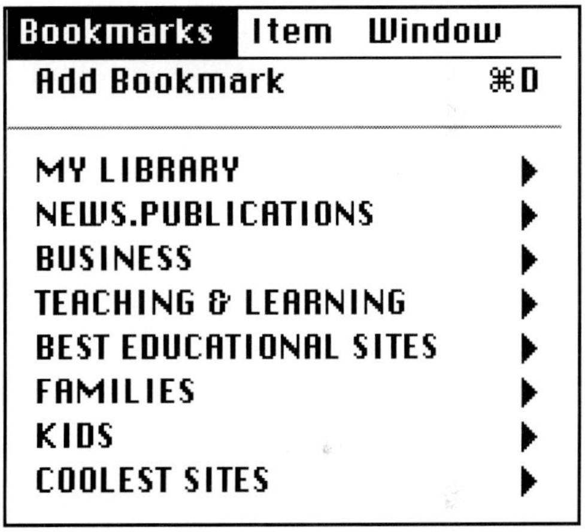

FIGURE 2.6
Netscape **Bookmark** menu

Bookmarks	Item	Window
Add Bookmark		⌘D
MY LIBRARY		▶
NEWS.PUBLICATIONS		▶
BUSINESS		▶
TEACHING & LEARNING		▶
BEST EDUCATIONAL SITES		▶
FAMILIES		▶
KIDS		▶
COOLEST SITES		▶

◙ **Add Bookmark:** Click on **Add Bookmark** to save this page in your bookmark list. Behind the scenes, Netscape saves the URL address so you can access this page by pointing-and-clicking on the item in your list.

◙ Bookmark Items: Below **Add Bookmark**, you will see a list of your saved pages. Point-and-click on any item to bring this page to your screen.

To view your bookmarks, add new bookmark folders, arrange the order of your bookmarks, or to do any editing, select the **Window** menu and choose **Bookmarks**.

Options Menu

The **Options** menu offers customization tools to personalize your use of Netscape Navigator. Several uses for these customization tools include:

- showing the toolbar buttons.
- showing the URL location of a page.
- showing the Directory buttons.
- automatic loading of images.
- selecting styles for pages to appear.
- selecting which Home Page you want to appear when you log onto Netscape.
- selecting link styles (colors).
- selecting your news server to interact with Usenet newsgroups.
- setting up e-mail on Netscape.

There are additional customization tools available that are more advanced. Refer to the Netscape online handbook for more information on **Options** and **Preferences**.

> **NOTE**
> Before you can use the e-mail and Usenet newsgroup tools available in Netscape, you will need to customize the **Mail and News Preferences**.

FIGURE 2.7
Netscape **Options** menu

- **General Preferences:** Presents tab buttons for selecting preferences. Each tab presents a panel for customizing Netscape's operations for your personal needs, preferences, and interests.

- **Mail and News Preferences:** Panel for entering information on your mail and news server, so you can use Netscape to send and receive e-mail and to participate in Usenet newsgroups.

- **Network Preferences:** Options for cache, network connections, and proxy configurations.

- **Security Preferences:** Panel for setting security features.

- **Show Toolbar:** If selected, the Toolbar buttons are visible on the Netscape page.

- **Show Location:** If selected, the URL location for the page is displayed.

- **Show Directory Buttons:** If selected, the Directory buttons are visible.

- **Show Java Console** (Windows only)**:** If selected, displays the Java Console window.

- **Auto Load Images:** If selected, images embedded into a page will be loaded automatically. If not checked, images can be loaded by clicking on the **Load Images** button. Deselecting this option increases the speed of downloading a page.

- **Document Encoding:** Lets you select which character set encoding a document uses when document encoding is either not specified or unavailable. The proportional and fixed fonts are selected using the **General Preferences/Fonts** panel.

- **Save Options:** Click on this option to save the changes you made to any of the above options.

Directory Menu

The **Directory** pull-down menu directs you to a few navigational aids to help you begin your Web exploration.

FIGURE 2.8
Netscape **Directory** menu

Directory	Window
Netscape's Home	
What's New?	
What's Cool?	
Netscape Galleria	
Internet Directory	
Internet Search	
Internet White Pages	
About the Internet	

- **Netscape's Home:** Takes you to the Netscape Home Page.

- **What's New:** Click on this item to see what's new on the Internet.

- **What's Cool:** Netscape's selection of interesting places to visit.

- **Netscape Galleria:** A showcase of Netscape customers who have built Net sites using Netscape Server software. Visit the Galleria to learn more about how to build and maintain innovative Web sites.

- **Internet Directory:** Same as the Internet Directory button. Links you to Internet directories for finding information and resources.

- **Internet Search:** Connects you to many of the best online search engines.

- **Internet White Pages:** Links you to tools to help you find people connected to the Internet.

- **About the Internet:** Links to resources to help you learn more about the Internet.

Window Menu

The **Window** menu makes it possible for you to navigate easily between your e-mail, Usenet news, and Bookmarks windows, and to see and visit places you have already traveled.

FIGURE 2.9
Netscape **Window** menu

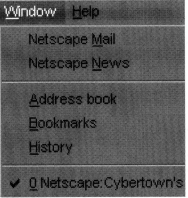

Window	Mon 12:
Netscape Mail	
Netscape News	
Address Book	
Bookmarks	⌘B
History	⌘H
GRAND CANYON National Park Home Page	

Macintosh **Window**

Window   Help
Netscape Mail
Netscape News
Address book
Bookmarks
History
✔ 0 Netscape:Cybertown's

Windows **Window**

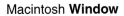 **Netscape Mail:** Click on this option to access the Netscape e-mail program.

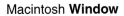 **Netscape News:** Click on this option to access the Usenet newsgroups.

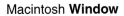 **Address Book:** Displays an Address Book window for use with the e-mail program.

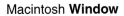 **Bookmarks:** Displays bookmarks and pull-down menus for working with or editing your bookmarks.

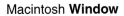 **History:** Displays a history list of the pages (their titles and URLs) that you have recently viewed. Select an item and press the **Go To** button (or double-click) to revisit the page.

Microsoft Internet Explorer

Now that you're familiar with Internet navigation using Netscape, you will be able to transfer that knowledge to the use of other Internet browsers. Most browsers have similar or the same navigational tools in the form of toolbar buttons and pull-down menus. Microsoft Internet Explorer is another widely used and highly sophisticated browser that is integrated with the Windows 95 operating environment. Explorer is the primary Internet browser for America Online (AOL) and CompuServe. Notice in Figure 2.10 how similar the navigational tools are to those of Netscape's Navigator.

FIGURE 2.10
Microsoft Internet Explorer window

Navigating With Internet Explorer

Toolbar buttons and pull-down menus are your Internet navigational tools when using Internet Explorer.

Toolbar Buttons

 Open: Accesses a dialog box for typing in URLs, documents, or folders for Windows to open.

 Print: Prints the page you are viewing.

 Send: Information services for using Microsoft's fax, e-mail, Netscape Internet transport, or Microsoft's Network Online Services.

 Back/Forward: Takes you either back to your previous page or forward to the next page in your history list.

 Stop: Stops the downloading of a Web page: text, images, video, or sound.

 Refresh: Brings a new copy of the current Explorer page from local memory to replace the one originally loaded.

 Open Start Page: Takes you back to the first opening page.

 Search the Internet: Click this button for a list of search services to help you find information on the Internet.

 Read Newsgroups: This option brings up a list of Usenet newsgroups available from your Internet provider or college/university.

Open Favorites: Click this button to see a list of your favorite URLs.

 Add to Favorites: Click on this button to add a favorite URL to your list.

 Use Larger/Smaller Font: Increase or decrease the size of the font on the page you are viewing.

 Cut: Removes what you have selected and places it on the clipboard.

 Copy: Copies the current selection to the computer's clipboard.

 Paste: Puts the current clipboard's contents in the document you are working on.

Pull-Down Menus

Pull-down menus offer navigational tools for your Internet exploration. Some of the options are similar to the toolbar buttons: File, Edit, View, Go, Favorites, Help.

NOTE

The pull-down menus will *not* be discussed or shown *unless* their functions differ significantly from the discussion of pull-down menus under Netscape Navigator.

File Menu

Explorer's **File** menu provides options for connecting to new Internet sites, printing Web pages, creating desktop shortcuts to your favorite Web pages, and to finding information about the page you are viewing.

FIGURE 2.11
Explorer's **File** pull-down menu

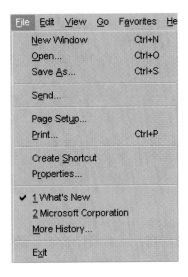

 **Create Shortcut:** Select this option to create a shortcut to the current page that will be placed on your desktop.

 **Properties:** Provides you with general information about the page you are viewing, including security information.

Edit Menu

The **Edit** menu offers cut, copy, and paste options as well as a find command for keywords searches.

FIGURE 2.12
Explorer's **Edit** menu

View Menu

The **View** menu options help you to determine how your Explorer page will appear. **Toolbar**, **Address Bar**, and **Status Bar** provide options for viewing or not viewing these Explorer tools.

FIGURE 2.13
Explorer's **View** menu
with active tools checked

Go Menu

The **Go** menu provides options for moving forward to the next page in your history list or backward to a previous page.

FIGURE 2.14
Explorer's **Go** menu
displaying navigational options

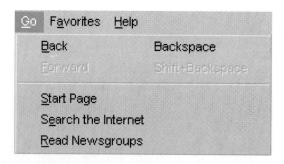

- **Start Page:** Takes you back to the opening page you started with.

- **Search the Internet:** Takes you to search tools for finding information on the Internet.

- **Read Newsgroups:** This option takes you to Explorer's news reader for Usenet newsgroups.

Favorites Menu

Explorer's **Favorites** list is the same as Netscape's Bookmarks or what other browser's refer to as a hotlist.

FIGURE 2.15
Explorer's **Favorites** menu

- **Add To Favorites:** Select this option to add the URL of a Web site to Explorer's Favorites list.

- **Open Favorites:** Use this option to select a URL for Explorer to open.

Help Menu

The **Help** menu provides help with using Internet Explorer.

FIGURE 2.16
Explorer's **Help menu**

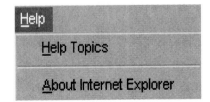

FIGURE 2.17

Explorer's **Help** Contents panel

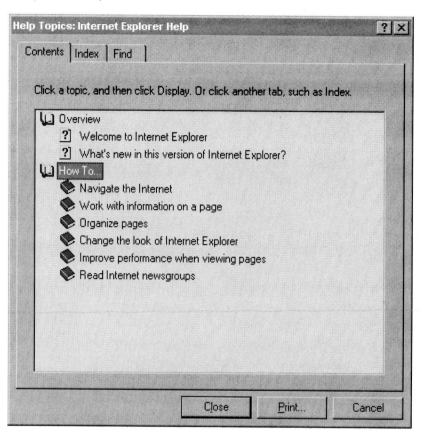

NOTE

Internet browsers such as Netscape Navigator and Internet Explorer support many additional capabilities such as electronic mail, Usenet newsgroups, Gopher, FTP, Telnet, and downloading and viewing image, video, and sound files. For a more in-depth discussion and practice using these features, refer to *Netscape Adventures—Step-by-Step Guide to Netscape Navigator and the World Wide Web* by Cynthia Leshin and published by Prentice Hall, 1997.

CHAPTER 3
Hands-on Practice

• •

In this chapter, you will practice using Netscape and/or Explorer for

- ➻ navigating the Internet.
- ➻ organizing and using bookmarks.
- ➻ exploring the Internet.

• •

> ## Practice 1:
> ## Browsing the Internet

In this guided practice you will use Netscape Navigator or Explorer to

- connect to World Wide Web sites and Home Pages;
- use pull-down menus and navigational toolbar buttons to navigate World Wide Web sites; and
- save bookmarks of your favorite pages.

1. *Log onto your Internet account.* When you have connected, open the Netscape Navigator or Explorer browser by double-clicking on the application icon.

Netscape Navigator Icon   Microsoft Explorer Icon

You will be taken to a Home Page. Notice the Location/Address URLs in Figure 3.1 and Figure 3.2. This Home Page may belong to Netscape Communications Corporation (**http://home.netscape.com**) or Microsoft (**http://www.microsoft.com**), or it may have been designed by your college or university. Look at the top of the Home Page in the Title Bar to see whose Home Page you are visiting.

URLs are a standard for locating Internet documents. Highlighted text on Netscape pages contains built-in URL information for linking to that information. You can also type in new URL text to link a page.

FIGURE 3.1

Netscape Navigator toolbar buttons

FIGURE 3.2

Microsoft Internet Explorer toolbar buttons

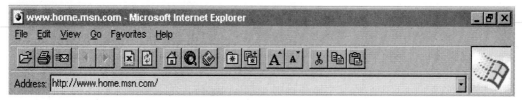

2. *Begin exploring* the World Wide Web by using Netscape's toolbar buttons and pull-down menus. Click on the **What's New** button. You will see a list of highlighted underlined links to Web sites. Click on a link and EXPLORE. HAVE FUN! If you are using Explorer, investigate the Home Page that you are viewing.

3. *Save your favorite pages* by making a bookmark or an addition to your Favorites List.

   When you find a page that you may want to visit at a later time, click on the pull-down menu, **Bookmarks**. Next, click on the menu item **Add Bookmark**. (Explorer—select the **Favorites** menu.)

   Click on the **Bookmarks** (**Favorites**) pull-down menu again. Notice the name of the page you marked listed below the **View Bookmarks** menu item. To view this page again, select the **Bookmarks** pull-down menu and click on the name of the page you saved.

4. Continue your exploration by clicking on the **What's Cool** button.

5. After you have linked to several pages, click on the **Go** pull-down menu. Notice the listing of the places you have most recently visited. If you want to revisit any of the pages you have already viewed, click on the name of the Web site.

Practice 2:
Organizing and Using Bookmarks

In this practice you will learn how to organize, modify, save, and move bookmark files. If you are using Explorer, save your favorite URLs by using either the **Favorites** button ⊞ or the **Favorites** menu.

Before you can organize and work with bookmark files, you must access Netscape's **Bookmark** window. There are two ways to access the **Bookmark** window:

- Go to the **Bookmarks** pull-down menu and select **Go To Bookmarks**; or

- Go to the **Window** pull-down menu and select **Bookmarks**.

1. *Organizing your bookmarks.* Before you begin saving bookmarks, it is helpful to consider how to *organize* saved bookmarks. Begin by thinking of categories that your bookmarks might be filed under such as Software, Business, Education, Entertainment, Research, and so forth. For each category make a folder. These are the steps for making your bookmark folders.

a. Go to the **Bookmarks** menu and select **Go To Bookmarks**, or go to the **Window** menu and select **Bookmarks**.

FIGURE 3.3

The Netscape **Bookmarks** window

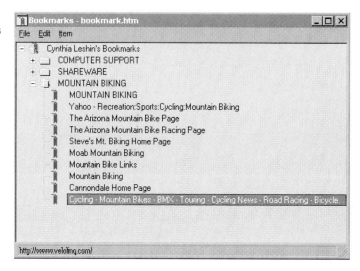

Notice the Web sites saved in the bookmarks folders in Figure 3.3. This Bookmarks window gives you three new menus for working with your bookmarks: **File**, **Edit**, and **Item**.

b. Create a new folder for a bookmark category by selecting the **Item** menu (Fig. 3.4).

FIGURE 3.4

Opened **Item** menu from within the Bookmarks window

34

c. Select **Insert Folder** (see Fig. 3.5).

FIGURE 3.5
Insert Folder window

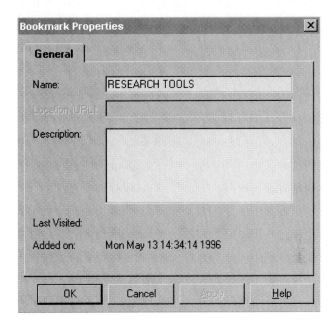

d. Type in the name of your folder in the Name dialog box.

e. Enter in description of the bookmark folder.

f. Click OK.

2. *Adding bookmarks to a folder.* Netscape provides an option for identifying which folder you would like to select to drop your bookmarks in.

a. Select the folder you would like to add your new bookmarks to by clicking on the name of the folder once. The folder should now be highlighted.

b. Go to the **Item** menu and select **Set to New Bookmarks Folder** shown near the bottom of Figure 3.4.

c. Go back to your Bookmark window and notice how this newly identified folder has been marked with a colored bookmark identifier. All bookmarks that you add will be placed in this folder until you identify a new folder.

3. *Modifying the name of your bookmark.* Bookmark properties contain the name of the Web site and the URL. You may want to change the name of the bookmark to indicate more clearly the information available at this site. For example, the bookmark name *STCil/HST Public Information* has very little meaning. Changing its name to *Hubble Space Telescope Public Information* is more helpful later when selecting from many bookmarks.

a. To change the name of a bookmark, select the bookmark by clicking on it once.

b. Go to the **Item** menu from within the Bookmark window.

c. Select **Properties**.

FIGURE 3.6
Properties window from Bookmark **Item** options

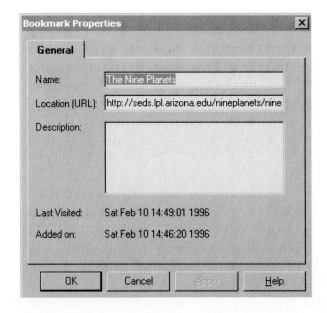

d. Enter in the new name for your bookmark by either deleting the text shown in Figure 3.6 or begin typing the new name when the highlighted text is visible.

e. Notice the URL for the bookmark; you can also enter in a new description for the URL.

4. *Making copies of your bookmarks for adding to other folders.* Occasionally you will want to save a bookmark in several folders. There are two ways to do this:

a. Select the bookmark that you would like to copy. Go to the **Edit** menu from within the Bookmark window and select **Copy**. Select the folder where you would like to place the copy of the bookmark. Go to the **Edit** menu and select **Paste**.

b. Make an alias of your bookmark by selecting **Make Alias** from the **Item** menu. When the alias of your bookmark has been created, move the alias bookmark to the new folder (see "NOTE").

> **NOTE**
> Bookmarks can be moved from one location to another by dragging an existing bookmark to a new folder.

5. *Deleting a bookmark.* To remove a bookmark:

a. Select the bookmark to be deleted by clicking on it once.

b. Go to the **Edit** menu from within the Bookmark window.

c. Choose either **Cut** or **Delete**.

6. *Exporting and saving bookmarks.* Netscape provides options for making copies of your bookmarks to either save as a backup on your hard drive, to share with others, or to use on another computer.

Follow these steps for exporting or saving your bookmarks to a floppy disk.

a. Open the **Bookmark** window.

b From within the Bookmark window, go to the **File** menu. Select **Save As.**

c. Designate where you would like to save the bookmark file—on your hard drive or to a floppy disk—in the **Save in** box.

FIGURE 3.7
Netscape Bookmark window for saving bookmark files

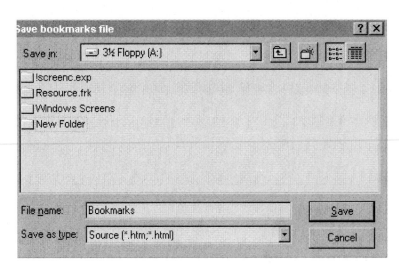

d. Enter in a name for your bookmark file in the **File name** dialog box.

e. Click **Save.**

7. *Importing Bookmarks.* Bookmarks can be imported into Netscape from a previous Netscape session saved on a floppy disk.

a. Insert the floppy disk with the bookmark file into your computer.

b. Open the **Bookmark** window.

c. From within the Bookmark window, go to the **File** menu and select **Import** (see Fig. 3.8).

d. Designate where the bookmark file is located: The **Look in** window displays a floppy disk or you can click on the scroll arrow to bring the hard drive into view.

FIGURE 3.8

Import window allows bookmark files from a floppy disk to be imported into your Netscape application

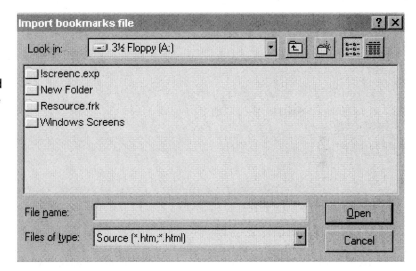

e. Click on **Open**. The bookmarks will now be imported into your Netscape bookmark list.

Practice 3:
Exploring the Internet With Your Web Browser

In this practice you will enter in URL addresses to link to World Wide Web (WWW) sites.

There are three options in Netscape for entering in a URL:

- the **Location** text field;
- the **File** menu—**Open Location;** or
- the **Open** toolbar button.

If you are using Explorer, select the **Open** button.

1. Select one of the above options to bring you to the window where you can enter your choice of URL text.

2. Listed below are several interesting Web sites to visit. Type a URL and EXPLORE. Remember to save your favorite sites as Bookmarks/ Favorites.

Awesome List: **http://www.clark.net/pub/journalism/awesome.html**

CityNet: **http://www.city.net**

ESPNetSportsZone: **http://espnet.sportzone.com**

NASA: **http://www.nasa.gov**

Time Warner Pathfinder:
http://www.timeinc.com/pathfinder/Greet.html

The White House: **http://www.whitehouse.gov**

Wired: **http://www.hotwired.com**

CHAPTER 4
Chatting on the Net

Although the Internet was created as a research network, it soon became popular for chatting and discussing work-related topics and hobbies. In this chapter you will learn how to communicate with others using

- listserv mailing lists.
- Usenet newsgroups.
- Internet Relay Chat (IRC).
- Internet phones.

People today are on the Internet because they value and enjoy the interactivity and the relationships they build within the virtual community of cyberspace. The way companies, institutions, and individuals communicate has changed. Internet communication involves five major services: electronic mail, electronic discussion groups (listservs and Usenet), Internet Relay Chat (IRC), Internet phones, and desktop Internet videoconferencing. E-mail and electronic discussion groups are delayed response media. IRC, Net phones, and desktop videoconferencing are real-time media. Net phones and videoconferencing are usually used for private conversations and IRC as a public forum. Electronic mail is most often used for private conversations; electronic discussion groups are used for public conversation.

Listserv Mailing Lists

With so much attention on the World Wide Web, many new Internet users miss learning about electronic mailing lists (also referred to as lists, listservs, or discussion groups) as an Internet resource for finding and sharing information. Electronic mailing lists began in the 1960s when scientists and educators used the Internet to share information and research. Early programs, known as *listservs*, ran on mainframe computers and used e-mail to send reports or studies to a large group of users.

Today, listservs perform the same function—the sharing of information. There are hundreds of special interest lists where individuals can join a virtual community to share and discuss topics of mutual interest.

What Is a Listserv Mailing List?

A *listserv* is the automated system that distributes electronic mail. E-mail is used to participate in electronic mailing lists. Listservs perform two functions:

- distributing text documents stored on them to those who request them, and
- managing interactive mailing lists.

Listservs and text documents

A listserv can be used to distribute information, in the form of text documents, to others. For example, online workshops may make their course materials available through a listserv. The listserv is set up to distribute the materials to participants at designated times. Other examples of documents available through a listserv include: a listing of all available electronic mailing lists, Usenet newsgroups, electronic journals, and books.

Interactive mailing lists

Interactive mailing lists provide a forum where individuals who share interests can exchange ideas and information. Any member of the group may participate in the resulting discussion. This is no longer a one-to-one communication like your e-mail, but rather a one-to-many communication.

Electronic mail written in the form of a report, article, abstract, reaction, or comment is received at a central site and then distributed to the members of the list.

How Does a Mailing List Work?

The mailing list is hosted by a college, university, or institution. The hosting institution uses its computer system to manage the mailing list.

Here are a few of the management functions of a listserv:

- receiving requests for subscriptions to the list;
- placing subscribers' e-mail addresses on the list;
- sending out notification that the name has been added to the list;
- receiving messages from subscribers;
- sending messages to all subscribers;
- keeping a record (archive) of activity of the list; and
- sending out information requested by subscribers to the list.

Mailing lists have administrators that may be either human or computer programs. One function of the administrator is to handle subscription requests. If the administrator is human, you can join the mailing list by communicating in English via an e-mail message. The administrator in turn has the option of either accepting or rejecting your subscription request. Frequently lists administered by humans are available only to a select group of individuals. For example, an executive board of an organization may restrict its list to its members.

Mailing lists administered by computer programs called listservs usually allow all applicants to subscribe. You must communicate with these computer administrators in listserv commands. For the computer administrator to accept your request, you must use the exact format required. The administrative address and how to subscribe should be included in the information provided about a list.

How to Receive Documents From a Listserv

E-mail is used to request text documents distributed by a listserv. The e-mail is addressed to the listserv *administrative address*. In the body of the message a command is written to request the document. The most common command used to request a document is "send" or "get." The command is then followed by the name of the document that you wish to receive. A command to request a list of interesting mailing lists might look like this:

"get" or "send" <name of document>

or

get new-list TOP TEN

How to Join a Listserv Mailing List

To join an interactive mailing list on a topic of interest, send an e-mail message to the list administrator and ask to join the list. Subscribing to an electronic mailing list is like subscribing to a journal or magazine.

- Mail a message to the journal requesting a subscription.

- Include the address of the journal and the address to which the journal will be mailed.

All electronic mailing lists work in the same way.

- E-mail your request to the list administrator at the address assigned by the hosting organization.

- Place your request to participate in the body of your e-mail where you usually write your messages.

- Your return address will accompany your request in the header of your message.

- Your subscription will be acknowledged by the hosting organization or the moderator.

- You will then receive all discussions distributed by the listserv.

- You can send in your own comments and reactions.

- You can unsubscribe (cancel your subscription).

The command to subscribe to a mailing lists looks like this.

subscribe <name of list> <*your name*>
or
subscribe EDUPAGE Cynthia Leshin

The unsubscribe command is similar to the subscribe command.

unsubscribe <name of list> *<your name>*

Active lists may have 50-100 messages from list participants each day. Less active mailing lists may have several messages per week or per month. If you find that you are receiving too much mail or the discussions on the list do not interest you, you can unsubscribe just as easily as you subscribed. If you are going away, you can send a message to the list to hold your mail until further notice.

> ## NOTE
>
> In Chapter 7 you will find the names of several electronic listservs (pg. 163) and Usenet newsgroups (pg. 174). Use this list to find listservs and newsgroups of interest to you.

Finding Listserv Mailing Lists
World Wide Web Sites for Finding Mailing Lists
Two of the best resources for helping you to find mailing lists are these World Wide Web sites:

http://www.liszt.com
http://www.tile.net/tile/listserv/index.html

E-Mail a Request for Listservs on a Topic
To request information on listserv mailing lists for a particular topic, send an e-mail message to

LISTSERV@vm1.nodak.edu

In the message body type: **LIST GLOBAL/*keyword***

To find electronic mailing lists you would enter:
LIST GLOBAL/management

Usenet Newsgroups

What Are Newsgroups?

In the virtual community of the Internet, a Usenet newsgroup is analogous to a cafe where people with similar interests gather from around the world to interact and exchange ideas. Usenet is a very large, distributed bulletin board system (BBS) that consists of several thousand specialized discussion groups. Currently there are over 20,000 newsgroups with 20 to 30 more added weekly.

You can subscribe to a newsgroup, scan through the messages, read messages of interest, organize the messages, and send in your comments or questions—or start a new one.

Usenet groups are organized by subject and divided into major categories.

Category	Topic Area
alt.	no topic is off limits in this alternative group
comp.	computer-related topics
misc.	miscellaneous topics that don't fit into other categories
news.	happenings on the Internet
rec.	recreational activities/hobbies
sci.	scientific research and associated issues
soc.	social issues and world cultures
talk.	discussions and debates on controversial social issues

In addition to these categories there are local newsgroups with prefixes that indicate their topics or localities.

Some newsgroups are moderated and reserved for very specific articles. Articles submitted to these newsgroups are sent to a central site. If the article is approved, it is posted by the moderator. Many newsgroups have no moderators and there is no easy way to determine whether a group is moderated. The only way to tell if a group is moderated is to submit an article. You will be notified if your article has been mailed to the newsgroup moderator.

What is the Difference Between Listserv Mailing Lists and Usenet Newsgroups?

One analogy for describing the difference between a listserv mailing list and a Usenet newsgroup is to compare the difference between having a few intimate friends over for dinner and conversation (a listserv) vs. going to a Super Bowl party to which the entire world has been invited (newsgroups). A listserv is a smaller, more intimate place to discuss issues of interest. A Usenet newsgroup is much larger and much more open to "everything and anything goes." This is not to say that both do not provide a place for valuable discussion. However, the size of each makes the experiences very different.

A listserv mailing list is managed by a single site, such as a university. Subscribers to a mailing list are automatically mailed messages that are sent to the mailing list submission address. A listserv would find it difficult to maintain a list for thousands of people.

Usenet consists of many sites that are set up by local Internet providers. When a message is sent to a Usenet site, a copy of the message that has been received is sent to other neighboring, connected Usenet sites. Each of these sites keeps a copy of the message and then forwards the message to other connected systems. Usenet can therefore handle thousands of subscribers.

One advantage of Usenet groups over a mailing list is that you can quickly read postings to the newsgroup. When you connect to a Usenet newsgroup and see a long list of articles, you can select only those that interest you. Unlike a mailing list, Usenet messages do not accumulate in your mailbox, forcing you to read and delete them. Usenet articles are on your local server and can be read at your convenience.

Netscape and Usenet Newsgroups

Netscape supports Usenet newsgroups. You can subscribe to a newsgroup, read articles posted to a group, and reply to articles. You can determine whether your reply is sent to the individual author of the posted article or to the entire newsgroup.

Netscape has an additional feature. Every news article is scanned for references to other documents called URLs. These URLs are shown as active hypertext links that can be accessed by clicking on the underlined words.

Newsgroups have a URL location. These URLs are similar, but not identical, to other pages. For example, the URL for a recreational backcountry newsgroup is **news:rec.backcountry**. The server protocol is **news:** and the newsgroup is **rec.backcountry.**

Newsgroups present articles along what is called a "thread." The thread packages the article with responses to the article. Each new response is indented one level from the original posting. A response to a response is indented another level. Newsgroups' threads, therefore, appear as outlines.

Buttons on each newsgroup page provide the reader with controls for reading and responding to articles. Netscape buttons vary depending on whether you are viewing a page of newsgroup listings or a newsgroup article.

Netscape News Window for Usenet News

To display the News window, go to the **Window** menu and select **Netscape News**.

FIGURE 4.1
The Netscape **News** window

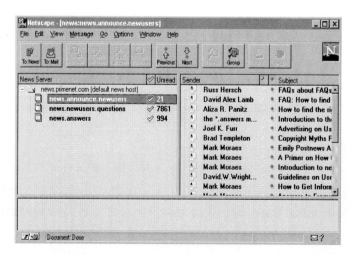

Notice that you have new options in the form of toolbar buttons and pull-down menus for receiving, reading, replying to, and sending messages to newsgroups. Netscape News works in much the same way as Netscape Mail.

Netscape News window buttons

To: News: Displays a Message Composition window for creating a new message posting for a newsgroup.

To: Mail: Displays a Message Composition window for creating a new mail message.

Re: Mail: Click on this button to reply to the current newsgroup message (thread) you are reading.

Re: Both: Displays a Message Composition window for posting a reply to the current message thread for the entire newsgroup and to the sender of the news message.

Forward: Displays the Message Composition window for forwarding the current news message as an attachment. Enter the e-mail address in the **Mail To** field.

Previous: Brings the previous unread message in the thread to your screen.

Next: Brings the next unread message in the thread to your screen.

Thread: Marks the message threads you have read.

Group: Marks all messages read.

Print: Prints the message you are reading.

Stop: Stops the current transmission of messages from your news server.

Netscape News Menus

When you select Netscape News you will receive not only new toolbar buttons but also different pull-down menus for interacting with the Netscape news reader: File, Edit, View, Message, Go, Options, Window, and Help.

NOTE

This guide does not give detailed information on using Netscape Navigator for Usenet newsgroups. For more information refer to *Netscape Adventures — Step-by-Step Guide to Netscape Navigator and the World Wide Web* by Cynthia Leshin.

For information on using Internet Explorer for newsgroups, see Explorer's online **Help** menu.

Reading Usenet News With Netscape Navigator

Netscape Navigator 2.0 provides four easy-to-access newsgroups.

- If you know the name of the newsgroup, type the URL in the location field of the Netscape main menu.

- From within the Netscape News window, go to the **File** menu and select **Add Newsgroup**. Enter the name of the newsgroup in the dialog box.

- From within the Netscape News window, go to the **Options** menu and select **Show All Newsgroups**. From this list, select a newsgroup and check the **Subscribe** box beside the newsgroup name.

- From a World Wide Web site, click on a link to a newsgroup or a newsgroup message.

FIGURE 4.2
Netscape News window
Options menu

Chats

Chats are programs that allow you to talk to many people at the same time from all over the world. Internet Relay Chat (IRC) is the most widely used program and has become one of the most popular Internet services. IRC has produced a new type of virtual community formed mainly by many young people. Although information may be exchanged on any topic and users can send and receive files, the primary use of IRC seems to be more social than business.

Many Internet access providers make IRC available to subscribers. Some institutions have IRC client programs installed. To connect to IRC, users merely type **irc**. If your institution does not have an IRC client program, you can Telnet to a public IRC server and chat from there. Some World Wide Web sites will have chat rooms for interactive discussion on topics of interest. For example, Time Warner's Pathfinder Web site has a chat room for discussing news of the day. Wired magazine has a chat room open for discussion.

After you have connected to an IRC, you will have to choose an online name, known as a *nickname,* to identify yourself. You will be known by your nickname. Next, you select a group or discussion topic, known as a *channel*, to join. There are any number of channels in IRC and any number of people within a channel. Some channels exist all the time; others come and go.

Conversations within chats are text-based. Users type in their messages line by line. As a line is being typed, others on the channel see the message. Messages cannot be edited before they are sent to others on the channel. Anyone on the channel can respond to a message as it is revealed on their computer screen by merely typing in their response line by line.

Commercial services such as America Online, CompuServe, Prodigy, and Microsoft Network offer chat rooms for their members to communicate and meet others who have similar interests. Chat rooms with these services can be public or private. Public rooms are created by the service provider and tend to have focused discussion topics. Some of these rooms are hosted, others are not. Some of these chat rooms are available on a regular basis, others are created for special events such as a guest who is online for a forum for several hours.

Private chat rooms are created by members and can hold between 2 and 25 or more registered online users. Private chat rooms may be used for a meeting or just a casual chat between friends. There is no way as to yet see a list of private chat rooms.

If you are interested in learning more about chats, check with your Internet service provider to see if IRC is available, or whether you will need to Telnet to an IRC client server. If you are a member of a commercial online service, check for information on its public and private chat rooms. To experience chat using the World Wide Web, explore these sites.

WebChat Broadcasting System **http://wbs.net**
HotWired **http://www.hotwired.com**
The Palace **http:www.thepalace.com**
Globe **http://globe1.csuglab.cornell.edu/global/homepage.html**

Internet Phones

The Internet has made possible the global transmission of text, graphics, sound, and video. Now, a new service has come upon the Internet shore making the real-time transmission of voice possible. Products known as Internet phones let you use your computer as a telephone. Internet phones are the hottest new Internet service to talk with another person anywhere in the world at no more than the cost of your local Internet access. Internet telephones can operate over cable, satellite, and other networks.

However, Internet phones are still in their infancy and not yet a substitute for conventional phones. At this stage in their development, they are still a novelty and far from practical to use as a business tool or for routine communication. To reach another person via the Internet phone, both parties need to be running the same software and be online at the same time when the call is made, otherwise the phone won't ring. Currently, most Internet phone software is similar to Internet Relay Chat programs that help users running the same program find and communicate with each other.

Part of the appeal of the Internet phone is the capability to talk to anyone in the world without the cost of a long distance phone call. For the monthly cost of an Internet account two people anywhere in the world can talk for as long and as often as they choose. When one compares this to the cost of national and international phone calls, many are willing to overlook the current limitations and difficulties imposed by this new technology on its users.

The capability and possibilities of the Internet phone have threatened traditional telecommunications companies. The American Carriers Telecommunication Association (ACTA) wants the Federal Communications Commission (FCC) to regulate Internet telephone products. Currently, there are no restrictions on the Net phone, but this could change as hearings are being conducted over the coming months. To keep up to date on these events visit these two Web sites: **http://www.von.org** or **http://www.netguide.com/net**

How Do I Talk to Someone Using an Internet Phone?

There are two ways that you can communicate with Internet users using Net phones:

- through a central server, similar to an Internet Relay Chat server
- connect to a specific individual by using their IP (Internet Protocol) address

Some Internet users have their own IP addresses; others are assigned an IP address every time they log on. Check with your Internet provider for information on your IP address.

What Do I Need to Use an Internet Phone?

Hardware

Before you can chat using Internet phones you will need the following hardware:

- a sound card for your Macintosh or Windows system
- speakers on your computer
- a microphone for your computer

Sound Card

To have a conversation where both parties can speak at the same time, you will need to have a sound card that supports full duplexing. Many Macintosh computers (including the Power Macs) support full-duplex sound. If you are using a PC, check your existing sound card. Full-duplex drivers are available if your sound card does not support full duplexing.

Speakers

The speakers that come with your computer are adequate for the current Net phones. The audio quality of this new technology is not yet what you are accustomed to with traditional telephones.

Microphone

Many computers come with microphones that will be suitable for use with the Internet phones. If you need to purchase a microphone, do not spend more than $10 to $15 on a desktop microphone.

Software

There are several Net phone products that were tested and recommended in the spring of 1996 by *Internet World* magazine.

- VocalTec's Internet Phone
- Quarterdeck Corp's Web Talk
- CoolTalk

Internet Phone (IPhone) was the first Net phone introduced to Internet users in early 1995. After the release and testing of many versions in 1995, the IPhone is considered one of the better Net phones with highly rated sound quality. IPhone is easy to use and resembles the chat environments. When you begin the program you log onto a variety of Internet servers and have the option of joining a discussion group. Once you have joined a group you can call an online user simply by double-clicking on the user's name. This capability is considered to be one of IPhone's strongest points.

The disadvantage of IPhone is that you cannot connect to a specific individual using their IP address. All connections must be made by first connecting to IPhone's IRC-style servers. Both individuals must be online at the same time and connected to the server.

Internet Phone has a free demo version with a one-week trial period. For more information visit their Web site at **http://www.vocaltec.com** or call (201) 768-9400.

Web Talk is the software program of choice for Internet users with their own IP address. To connect to a specific individual, just enter their IP address. The person you are trying to connect with must also be online at the same time. To talk with other online users, connect to WebTalk's server. To learn more about WebTalk visit its Web site at **http://www.webtalk,qdeck.com** or call (301) 309-3700.

CoolTalk is distributed by Netscape Communications Corp. and has a cool feature, the whiteboard, that sets it apart from other Internet phone programs. The whiteboard option becomes available after you have connected to another individual. (Connections are made by either logging onto their global server or entering in an individual's IP address.) The whiteboard begins as a blank window. Using standard paint program tools you can enter text, sketch out ideas, draw, or insert graphics. The whiteboard makes this Net phone a most attractive program for Internet business users.

Netscape Navigator 3.0 incorporates Internet telephone communication capabilities.

NOTE

Keep an eye on Intel's Internet-Phone. This software is free and has the advantage of allowing users to talk with those using different phone software. MCI has plans to launch a service in partnership with Intel to provide telephone and video services to businesses. **http://www.intel.com**

NOTE

You can also chat across the Internet using videoconferencing programs such as CU-SeeMe. This program makes it possible for interaction with one individual, small groups, or hundreds in a broadcast. Not only do you hear individuals, but you also can see them in full color on your computer monitor. This program has a whiteboard feature for document collaboration.

CU-SeeMe runs on Windows or Macintosh over a 28.8 modem. If you have a 14.4 modem only, audio is possible. To learn more, visit their Web site at **http://www.cu-seeme.com/iw.htm** or call (800) 241-PINE.

CHAPTER 5
Finding Information and Resources on the Internet

• •

In this chapter, you will learn how to find information and resources on the Internet. You will be using search engines, search directories, and Internet resource collections to find information in the management field. You will learn about the following search tools:

- ❧ Yahoo (search directory)
- ❧ Magellan and Galaxy (search directories)
- ❧ Excite (search engine and search directory)
- ❧ Alta Vista (search engine)
- ❧ InfoSeek (search engine and search directory)
- ❧ Open Text (search engine)

• •

The Internet contains many tools that speed the search for information and resources. Research tools called "search directories" and "search engines" are extremely helpful.

Search Directories
Search directories are essentially a subject index of Web sites. They also have searching options. When you connect to their page, you will find a query box for entering in keywords. The search engine at these sites searches only for keyword matches in the directories' databases.

Search Engines
Search engines are different from search directories in that they search World Wide Web sites, Usenet newsgroups, and other Internet resources to find matches to your descriptor keywords. Many search engines also rank the results according to a degree of relevancy. Most search engines provide options for advanced searching to refine your search.

Basic Guidelines for Using Search Tools

Search directories and search engines are marvelous tools to help you find information on the Internet. Search directories are often the best places to begin a search, frequently providing more relevant returns on a topic than a search engine which may generate a high proportion of irrelevant information. Therefore, it is essential that you use several search tools for your research.

The basic approach to finding information involves the following steps:

1. Use search directories such as Yahoo (**http://www.yahoo.com**), Excite (**http://www.excite.com**), Galaxy (**http://galaxy.einet.net/ galaxy.html**), Magellan (**http://magellan.mckinley.com)** or Infoseek (**http://guide.infoseek.com**) to search for the information under a related topic or category. Explore the links that seem relevant to your topic, and make bookmarks of the ones you would like to investigate further. Look for one site that has a large collection of links on your topic. This is the resource goldmine that you are looking for.

2. Use search engines to further research your topic by determining one or more descriptive words (keywords) for the subject. Enter your keywords into the search dialog box.

3. Determine how specific you want your search to be. Do you want it to be broad or narrow? Use available options to refine or limit your search. Some search engines permit the use of boolean operators (phrases or words such as "and," " or," and "not" that restrict a search). Others provide HELP for refining searches, and some have pull-down menus or selections to be checked for options or advanced options.

4. Submit your query.

5. Review your list of hits (a search return based on a keyword).

6. Adjust your search based on the information returned. Did you receive too much information and need to narrow your search? Did you receive too little or no information and need to broaden your keywords?

Yahoo

Yahoo is one of the most popular search tools on the Internet and is an excellent place to begin your search. Although Yahoo is more accurately described as a search directory, this Web site has an excellent database with search options available. Yahoo can be accessed from the Netscape Search Directory button, or by entering this URL: **http://www.yahoo.com**

There are two ways to find information using Yahoo: search through the subject index, or use the built-in search engine.

Yahoo Subject Index

When you connect to Yahoo, you will see a list of subjects or directories. Select the topic area that best fits your search needs. Follow the links until you find the information you are searching for.

Using Yahoo to Search for Information

Follow these steps to use Yahoo to search for information:

1. Begin by browsing the subject directory. For example, if you were searching for information on "how businesses use the Internet to communicate with customers," you would first select the *Business and Economy* directory and then follow the links to *Companies*. Explore, and see how companies are using the Internet to provide interactive communication services.

2. Yahoo's search engine can also be used to find information. Enter a descriptive keyword for your subject, one that uniquely identifies or describes what you are looking for. It is often helpful to do a broad search first, though results often provide information on the need to change descriptive keywords or to refine your query.

   Perhaps you know the name of a company, such as Silicon Graphics, that takes advantage of the Internet as an interactive medium to provide entertaining consumer content and services. Enter the name of the company, in this case "Silicon Graphics" (see Fig. 5.1).

3. Click on the **Search** button and review your query results (see Fig. 5.2).

FIGURE 5.1

Yahoo search form and subject index in which the keywords *Silicon Graphics* have been entered

FIGURE 5.2

Yahoo search results from the keywords *Silicon Graphics*

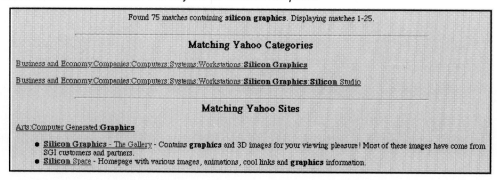

4. You may now want to refine your search. Most search engines have options for advanced searching using boolean logic or more carefully constructed database queries. Review the search page for **Options** or **Advanced Options**. When using Yahoo, click on the **Options** button.

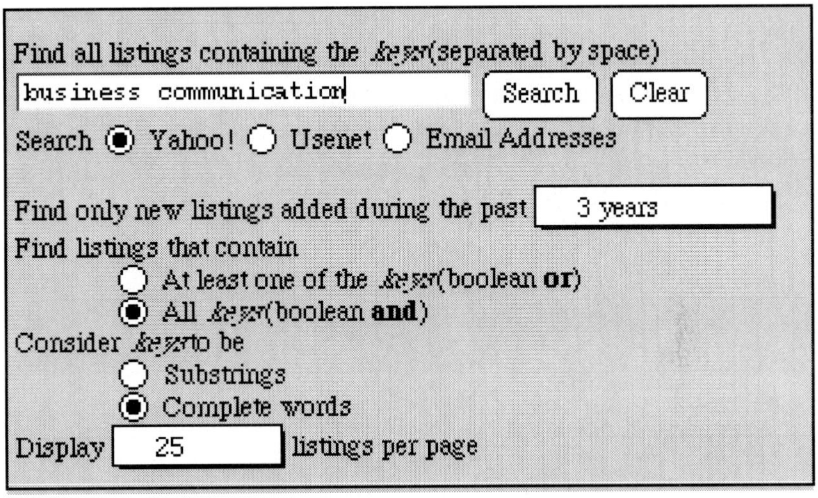

FIGURE 5.3
Yahoo **Options** for refining a search

Find all listings containing the *keys* (separated by space)

| business communication| | Search | Clear |

Search ● Yahoo! ○ Usenet ○ Email Addresses

Find only new listings added during the past | 3 years |

Find listings that contain
 ○ At least one of the *keys* (boolean **or**)
 ● All *keys* (boolean **and**)
Consider *keys* to be
 ○ Substrings
 ● Complete words
Display | 25 | listings per page

If you are using two keywords, do you want Yahoo to look for either word (boolean **or**), both keywords (boolean **and**), or all words as a single string? For example, in the search for "business communication" select boolean **and** because you want to find resources that contain both words "business" **and** "communication" in their titles (see Fig. 5.3). Otherwise the search would be too broad and would find all resources that contained either of the keywords "business" **or** "communication."

5. Further limit or expand your search by selecting Substrings or Complete words. For example, with your *business communication* search, you would select the search option for *Complete words,* or Yahoo treats the word as a series of letters rather than a whole word. A research return using substrings would include all incidences where both the words *business* and *communication* appeared in any form.

6. Determine the number of matches you want returned for your search.

7. Submit your query.

8. Review your return list of hits and adjust your search again if necessary.

9. Review your return list for other descriptive words that have been used when summarizing search results. For example, when using keywords "business communication," search result summaries produced other important descriptive words such as "Internet communication" and "computer-mediated communication."

10. Conduct a search using other descriptive words.

Magellan and Galaxy

Magellan (**http://magellan.mckinley.com**) and Galaxy (**http://galaxy.einet.net/galaxy.html**) are two other excellent search directories. Magellan provides options for narrowing or expanding your search by selecting sites rated from one to four stars (four stars being the most restricted). You can also restrict your search by excluding sites with mature content by searching for "Green Light" sites only (a green light will be displayed next to the review).

FIGURE 5.4
Home page for Magellan with options for specializing your search

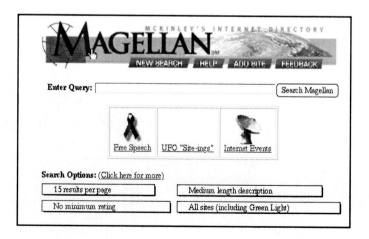

Excite

Excite provides the fullest range of services of all the search tools. Excite searches scanned Web pages and Usenet newsgroups for keyword matches and creates summaries of each match. Excite also has a Web directory organized by category. Excite consists of three services:

- **NetSearch**—comprehensive and detailed searches

- **NetReviews**—organized browsing of the Internet, with site evaluations and recommendations

- **Excite** Bulletin—an online newspaper with reviews of Internet resources, a newswire service from Reuters, and its own Net-related columns

Excite offers two different types of search options: concept-based searching and keyword searching. The search engines described thus far have used keyword search options. Keyword searches are somewhat limited due to the necessity of boolean qualifiers to limit searches.

Concept-based searching goes one step beyond keyword searches—finding what you mean and not what you say. Using, the phrase "communicating with media," a concept-based search will find documents that most closely match this phrase. Excite is available at: **http://www.excite.com**

Searching With Excite

1. Type in a phrase that fits your information need.
   Be as specific as you can, using words that uniquely relate to the information you are looking for, not simply general descriptive words. For example, for your media communication search enter the following phrase: *communicating with media*

FIGURE 5.5

Excite Web page displaying concept-based search
using the phrase *communicating with media*

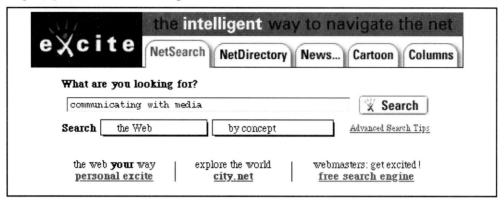

2. If the search result does not contain the information you are looking for, or if the returns provide too much irrelevant information, use the Advanced Search options.

3. Advanced features include the use of a plus sign (**+**) in front of a search word to ensure that all the returns contain that word. Use a minus sign (**-**) in front of a search word and Excite will make sure that NO documents contain the word. Excite also supports the use of boolean operators (**AND, OR, NOT**).

4. Excite lists 10 search results at a time in decreasing order of confidence. Each result lists a title, a URL, and a brief summary of the document. The percentage to the left of the return is the confidence rating (Figure 5.7), with 100% being the highest confidence rating attainable. To see the next listing of documents related to your phrase or keywords, click the "next documents" button. Click the "sort by site" button to view the Web sites that have the most pages relevant to your search.

FIGURE 5.6
Search results for *communicating with media*
(concept-based search) with a percentage
of confidence rating for finding relevant information

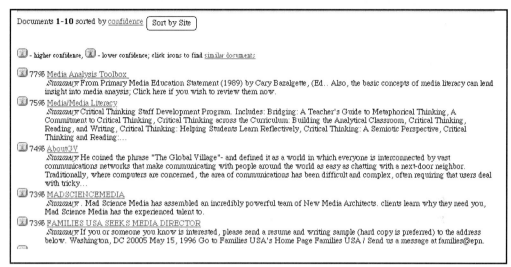

FIGURE 5.7
Excite search showing
percentage of
confidence rating

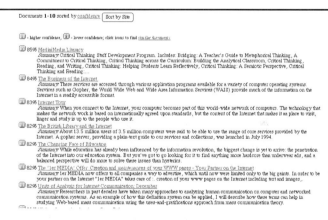

Alta Vista

Digital's Alta Vista is considered one of the best search engines currently available, with one of the largest Web-search databases. Alta Vista's searches are consistently more comprehensive than any of the other search tools. Although you will spend a great deal of time browsing your search results, you will be provided with as much information as possible on a search query. **http://altavista.digital.com**

Use Alta Vista to search for information on "interactive advertising." Conduct two searches: a simple query and an advanced query.

1. A simply query is conducted by entering in keywords or phrases. Do not use AND or OR to combine words when doing a simple query. For this query, type in the phrase: *interactive advertising*

FIGURE 5.8
Alta Vista Home Page

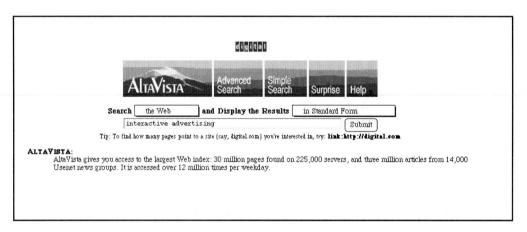

2. Alta Vista's advanced options use the binary operators AND, OR, and NEAR and the unary operator NOT. For more information on the advanced options, click on the *Help for Advanced Options*.

   To conduct a more refined search using Alta Vista's advanced options, enter the following words: *interactive AND advertising AND Internet*.

FIGURE 5.9
Alta Vista advanced options search using the binary operator AND

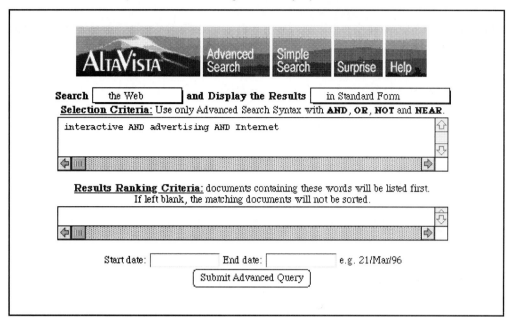

InfoSeek

InfoSeek is a professional service provided by InfoSeek Corporation. In 1995, InfoSeek introduced its easy-to-use search services to subscribers for a monthly subscription fee. Because of its popularity, the services have been expanded to include two new options: InfoSeek Guide and InfoSeek Professional.

InfoSeek Guide is the free service that integrates the latest search technology with a browsable directory of Internet resources located on World Wide Web sites, Usenet newsgroups, and other popular Internet resource sites. Users can choose to use the search engine and enter keywords or phrases, or browse the navigational directories.

Visit the InfoSeek Guide site and try these tools for finding Internet information and resources. **http://guide.infoseek.com**

InfoSeek Professional is a subscription-based service that offers individuals and business professionals comprehensive access to many Internet resources such as newswires, publications, broadcast programs, business, medical, financial and government databases. The difference between InfoSeek Guide and InfoSeek Professional is the capability to conduct more comprehensive searches and to have options for refining and limiting searches. For example, you can conduct a search query by just entering in a question such as "How are companies using the Internet for communication with customers?" You can also limit your query to just the important words or phrases that are likely to appear in the documents you are looking for:"communicating" with "customers" using the "Internet."

By identifying the key words or phrases (**communicating**, **customers**, and **Internet**) with quotation marks, your search accuracy is greatly enhanced.

InfoSeek Professional offers a free trial period. To learn how to perform the most efficient search, link to InfoSeek's information on search queries and examples. **http://professional.infoseek.com**

FIGURE 5.10
InfoSeek guide for information and resources

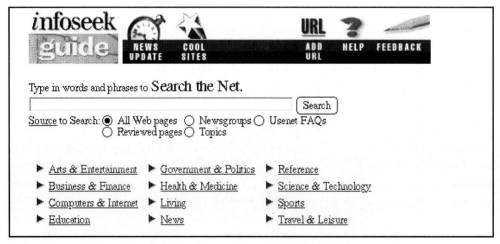

Open Text

Open Text has one of the most comprehensive collections of search tools and is one of the best designed search engines on the Internet. **http://www.opentext.com**

Open Text offers many search options:

- simple query on words;
- a power search using up to five operators between terms (*and, or, not, but not, near,* and *followed by*);
- options to create your own weighted search;
- results scored by relevancy; and
- an option to show a report of where Open Text found your search matches.

Open Text produces better returns on your search if you break up a phrase into keywords. For example, when "using the Internet to communicate with customers" was entered, Open Text reported many irrelevant results. When the query was changed to the individual search terms, "business" "communication" and "media" a large number of relevant results was displayed.

FIGURE 5.11
Open Text page showing query entered with
three search terms: "business" "communication" "media"

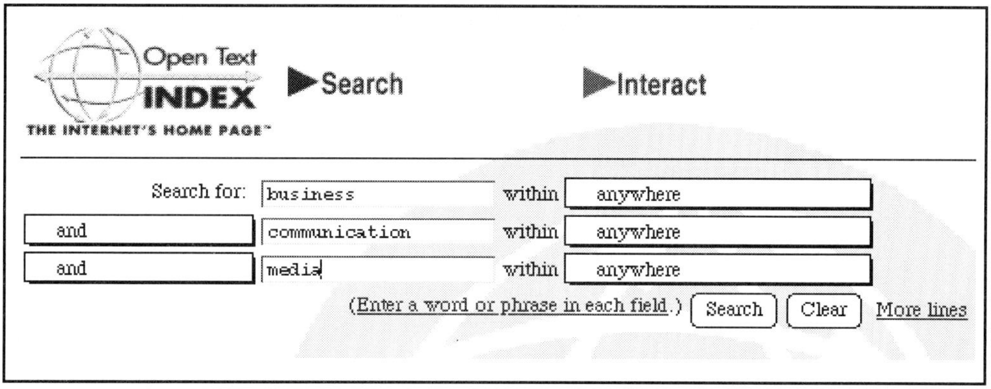

Search Guidelines—The Treasure Hunt

- Begin your search by looking for relevant documents in search directories such as Yahoo, Excite, Galaxy, Magellan, and Infoseek.

- Use search engines to further your search. Run a search using descriptive keywords. These preliminary searches provide you with an overview of what is available on your topic and how effective the engine was in finding the information you are looking for.

- Use these preliminary results to refine your search. Review results for other descriptive words that have been used in search summaries.

- Check for advanced search options in the search engine you are using. Some may offer options using boolean qualifiers such as AND or OR to limit your search. Others may have you enter a (+) sign in front of all words that must be included in the search.

- Use more than one search engine. You will find that search results vary depending on which search tool you use.

- Think of related or associated places that might have information on your topic. For example, in researching the Olympics, in addition to a search using the keyword "Olympics," you might research the name of the city where the Olympic games are to be held, the station televising the games, and other news or sports channels with Web sites such as ESPN. Your search engine(s) may not find some of the best Web sites from the television or news stations.

- When you find a Web site, spend time exploring the links. Internet research involves many links and going deeper into them. You will find buried treasures at the end of many linked pathways. The information goldmines are frequently not the ones found by your search engine or by preliminary checking of a few links. The true treasures come from much exploration and digging deep within Web links.

Using the Internet for Business Research

Searching for information is like a treasure hunt. Unless a researcher has knowledge of all the resources and tools available, then the search for useful information may be a time consuming and frustrating process. In this section you will learn about resources on the Internet that will facilitate the search for valuable business information on the Net. Careful thought about the desired knowledge sought, where the best place is to begin to look for that knowledge, and extensive exploring and searching in layers of Web links, usually provides the desired reward—the gold nugget Web site.

Your tools for conducting a business search include
- search engine(s)
- search directories
- business related collections or directories

Search Engines

Search engines can be frustrating to use when searching for business resources and may not prove to be the best Internet resources to begin with. Although these search tools have advanced options for refining and limiting a search, business researchers may find that finding the desired information is not easy and that search results frequently provide a high percentage of irrelevant and useless information. For example, using a search engine such as Alta Vista for a search with the keywords *business management* provides a large number of irrelevant returns. In this search return, Alta Vista found 500,000 occurrences of the words *business* and *management*. Many of the occurrences of these words were in job listings or companies that were advertising their services (see Fig. 5.13).

FIGURE 5.12
Alta Vista search using keywords *business* and *management*

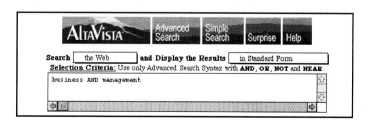

FIGURE 5.13

Alta Vista search return with keywords *business* and *management*

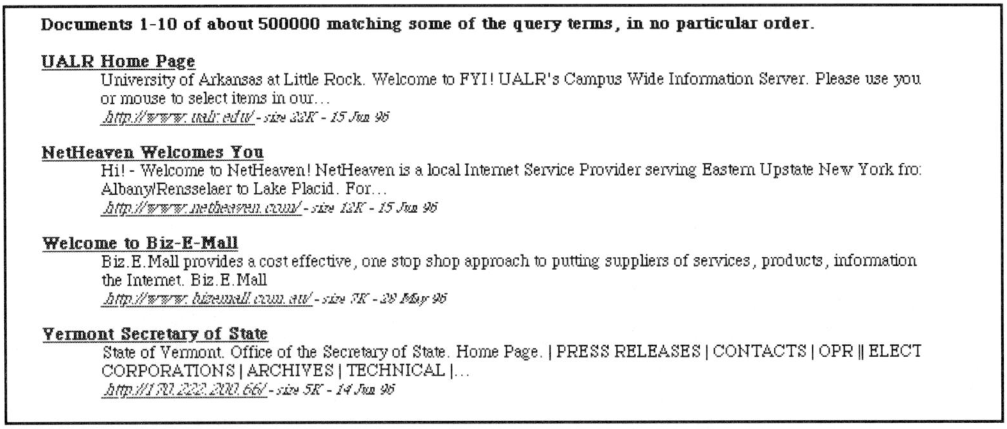

Documents 1-10 of about 500000 matching some of the query terms, in no particular order.

UALR Home Page
University of Arkansas at Little Rock. Welcome to FYI! UALR's Campus Wide Information Server. Please use you or mouse to select items in our...
http://www.ualr.edu/ - *size 33K - 15 Jun 96*

NetHeaven Welcomes You
Hi! - Welcome to NetHeaven! NetHeaven is a local Internet Service Provider serving Eastern Upstate New York fro: Albany/Rensselaer to Lake Placid. For...
http://www.netheaven.com/ - *size 12K - 15 Jun 96*

Welcome to Biz-E-Mall
Biz.E.Mall provides a cost effective, one stop shop approach to putting suppliers of services, products, information the Internet. Biz.E.Mall
http://www.bizemall.com.au/ - *size 5K - 28 May 96*

Vermont Secretary of State
State of Vermont. Office of the Secretary of State. Home Page. | PRESS RELEASES | CONTACTS | OPR || ELECT CORPORATIONS | ARCHIVES | TECHNICAL |...
http://170.222.200.66/ - *size 5K - 14 Jun 96*

Other searches using search engines and keywords such as *teams*, *management of change*, *motivation*, *decision making*, and *stress* also provided many useless and irrelevant returns. Most of the returns were, again, companies advertising their services.

Search Directories

Search tools such as Yahoo, Galaxy, Excite, and Infoseek have search directories that are good places to begin business research. Search directories categorize Internet information into subject categories. Usually, you will be able to find a related category for what you are searching for. In this example, we will begin with the *Business* category in Yahoo.

FIGURE 5.14

Yahoo Home Page showing information categories
http://www.yahoo.com

Click on the link to *Business and Economy* to view the Yahoo's categorized business resources.

FIGURE 5.15

Yahoo's Business and Economy categories

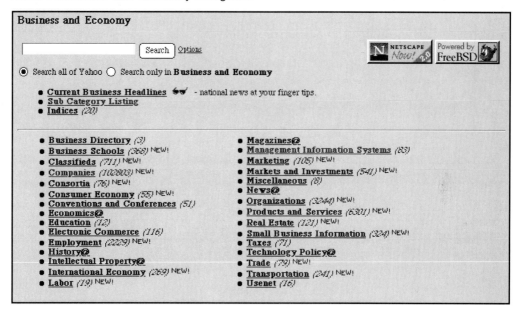

Select the link to *Management Information Systems*.

FIGURE 5.16

Yahoo resources for Management Information Systems

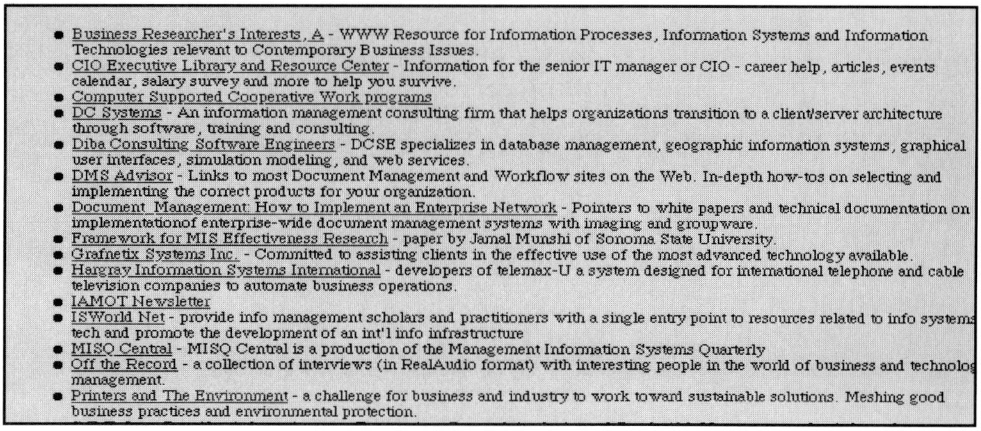

The search returns for this search are more relevant. Listed are Web sites that appear to be worth investigating. The returns are not heavily filled with commercial Web sites.

NOTE

The information returned in search directories tends to be less commercial. Searching directories usually provides a number of useful and relevant Internet resources to use as a starting point.

Yahoo's search directory also has options to do a keyword search—a search in Yahoo's entire database or just in the database which you are viewing. In this case, Business and Economy.

Galaxy—Search Directory—http://galaxy.einet.net/galaxy.html
Another search directory is Galaxy. Galaxy has links to many excellent business resources when you link to their business directory. After connection to the Galaxy Directory, select *Business General Resources*.

FIGURE 5.17
Galaxy Business—Directories listing

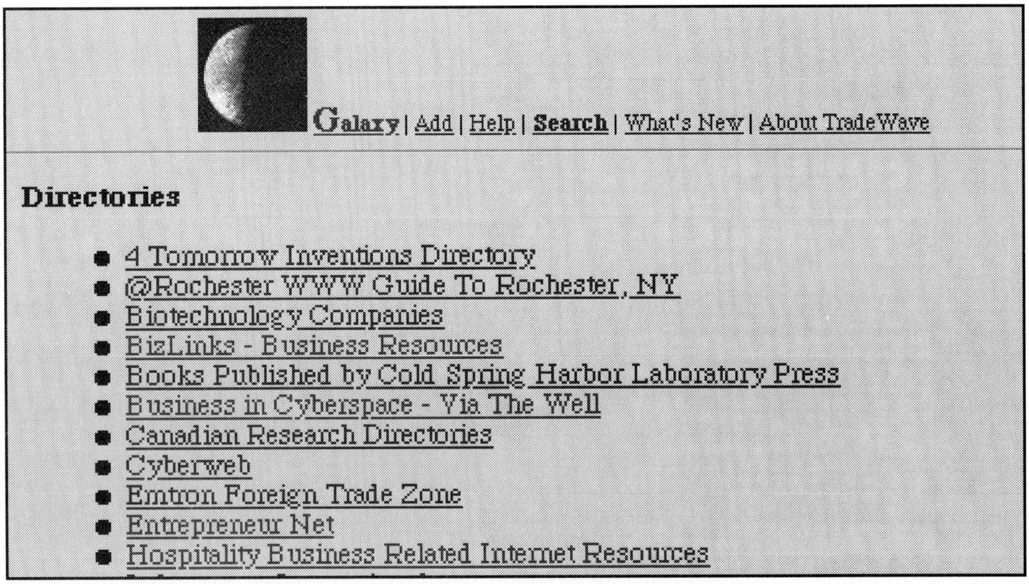

Galaxy | Add | Help | **Search** | What's New | About TradeWave

Directories

- 4 Tomorrow Inventions Directory
- @Rochester WWW Guide To Rochester, NY
- Biotechnology Companies
- BizLinks - Business Resources
- Books Published by Cold Spring Harbor Laboratory Press
- Business in Cyberspace - Via The Well
- Canadian Research Directories
- Cyberweb
- Emtron Foreign Trade Zone
- Entrepreneur Net
- Hospitality Business Related Internet Resources

Galaxy has many excellent links in their business directory section. Several resources that have valuable business information links include BizLinks and Nijenrode Business Resources. Select Nijenrode Business Resources link.

FIGURE 5.18
Nijenrode Business Resources page

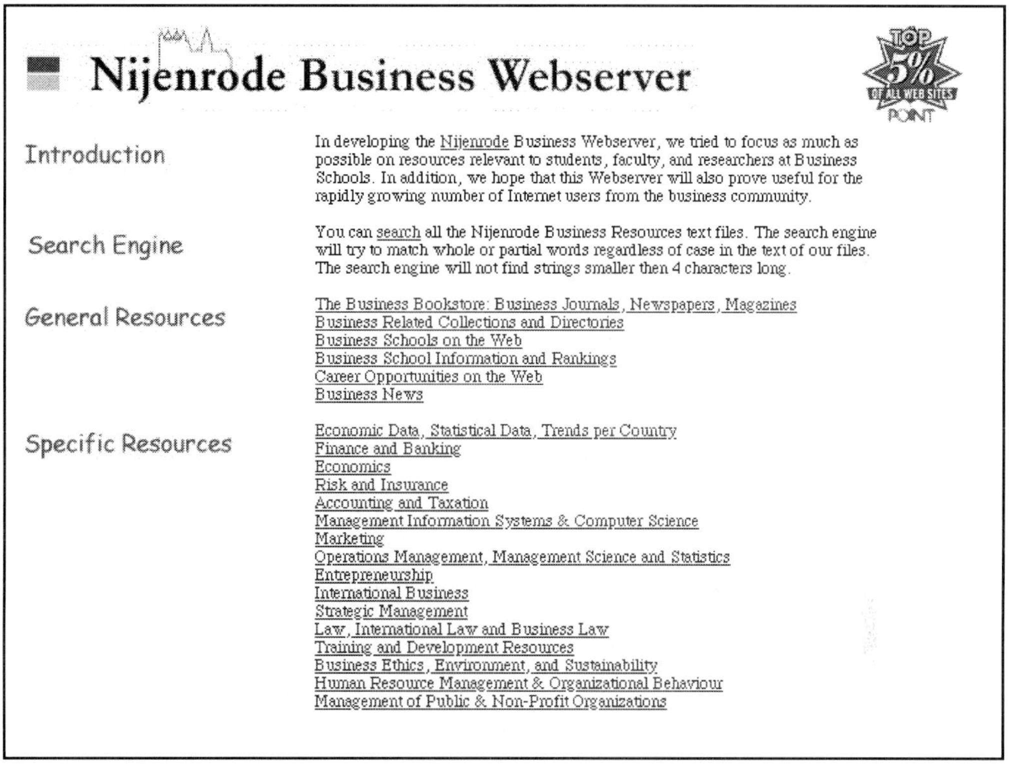

This Web server has many excellent links for business resources to explore. This is where the excitement of the treasure hunt begins. Once you have found a valuable information directory, such as the Nijenrode Business Webserver, spend time exploring links and saving bookmarks of interesting sites. At this point, when you begin exploring links, it is easy to get lost in cyberspace. You will find it helpful to organize your travel with the use of bookmarks.

Select the link to *Strategic Management*.

FIGURE 5.19

Link to Nijenrode Strategic Management resources

Nijenrode also has a search option for finding information on their Webserver. Notice the search link in the upper right corner (see Fig.5.19).

After exploring the resources on the Nijenrode server, go back to Galaxy and see if there are other links of interest to explore. One link that seems interesting is listed under Galaxy's Periodicals, *The Wall Street Journal* Interactive Edition at **http://wsj.com**

FIGURE 5.20

The Wall Street Journal Interactive Edition page

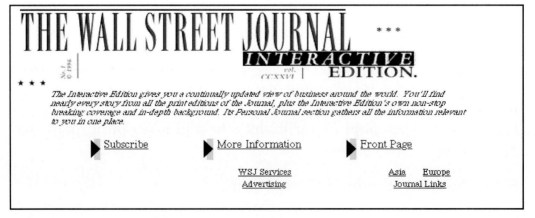

The Wall Street Journal Interactive Edition provides a continually updated view of business around the world.

Excite—Subject Directory—http://www.excite.com

Another excellent subject directory to investigate is Excite. After connecting to Excite, click on **NetDirectory**. Next select the **Business** index.

FIGURE 5.21

Excite's Business Management resources found in the NetDirectory

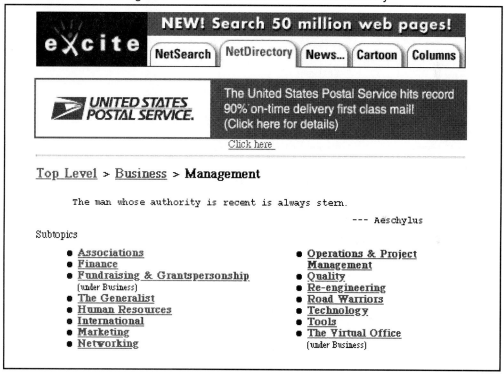

The Management directory found in the Business index has many excellent categories to explore: Human Resources, International, Marketing, Operations and Project Management, Quality, Re-Engineering, and more.

InfoSeek—Subject Directory—http://guide.infoseek.com

InfoSeek has a free search service that includes this excellent subject directory. Select the link to *Business and Finance*.

FIGURE 5.22

InfoSeek's Business and Finance page

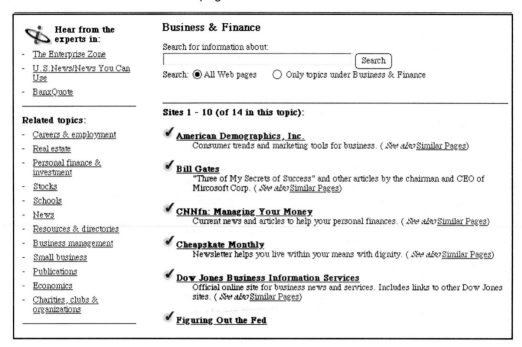

The business resource links are different in InfoSeek from those of Yahoo, Galaxy, and Excite. Notice the related topics on the left side of the page. These are links to topics related to *Business and Finance*. This page also includes links to Internet sites—listed on the right side of the page—related to the topic.

Exploration of these four search directories (Yahoo, Galaxy, Excite, InfoSeek) illustrates that each has very different information in their database. Access to this information also varies as does the quality of the information.

Compare the resources in *business management* to the other three search directories by selecting *Business Management*.

FIGURE 5.23

Business Management resources found in InfoSeek

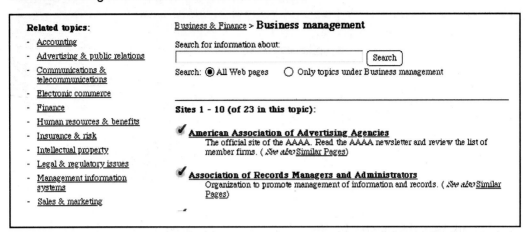

Business Related Collections and Directories

There are many other directories that provide links to business resources. You will find that frequently a college class or a professor may maintain a Web site with valuable resource links. For example, an excellent Business Web site called Madalyn is maintained by the University of Delaware MBA program.

FIGURE 5.24

Madalyn
Home Page

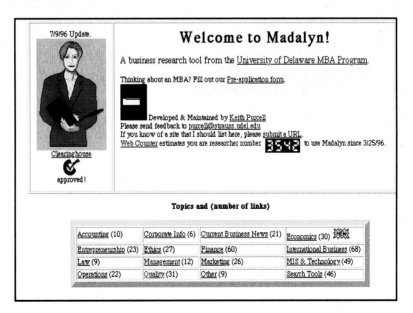

Visit Madalyn at **http://www.udel.edu/alex/mba/main/netdir2.html** to explore links to accounting, corporate information, economics, entrepreneurship, ethics, finance, international business, management, marketing, quality, and more.

Listed below are Internet business sites that provide excellent and valuable business information.

Business Research Sites

Wall Street Research Net
http://www.wsrn.com

FIGURE 5.25
Wall Street Research Net Home Page

IMPORTANT SURVEY INPUT NEEDED
(The Financial Site User Survey)

Wall Street Research Net consists of over 110,000 links to help professional and private investors perform fundamental research on actively traded companies and mutual funds and locate important economic data that moves markets.

Find out <u>What's New</u> - Last updated July 17, 1996

Please take the time to <u>register</u>. Thank You.

GRANT'S Interest Rate Observer is now online bringing analysis and commentary to help make better investment decisions. GRANT'S Interest Rate Observer provides an extraordinary breadth of coverage: GRANT'S is an independent, skeptical and literate voice on the subjects of credit, interest rates, the bond markets, commodities, real estate and monetary trends.

Select the *Wall Street Research Net* link to view your research options.

FIGURE 5.26
Areas of research for Wall Street Research Net

To research a company, click the box *Research A Company*.

FIGURE 5.27
Wall Street Research—a company search tool

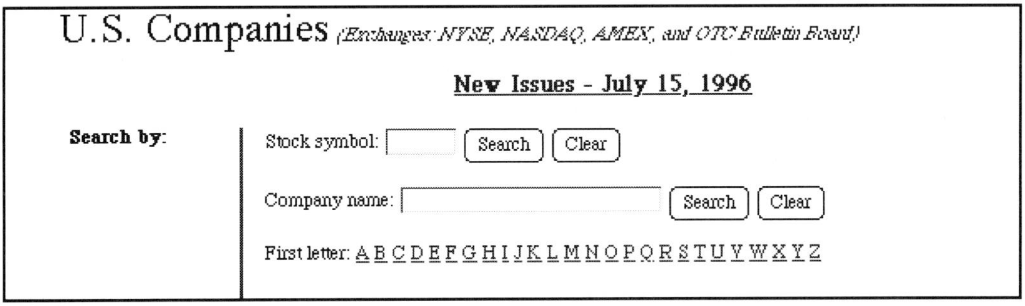

Enter the name of a company on which you are searching for information. For this example, we will enter in Netscape Communication Corporation. The next screen displays the options for information on Netscape.

FIGURE 5.28
Options for researching a company

NETSCAPE COMMUNICATIONS CORP
(NASDAQ : NSCP)

Home Page
Current Quote
Silicon Investor Company Profile
SEC Filings (NETSCAPE COMMUNICATIONS)
1995 Annual Report
StockMaster Chart
Press Releases
Money & Investing Briefing Book
You will need a subscription to Money & Investing to have access to the **Briefing Book**.
Company News
Yahoo! Company Profile
Stock Graph
Search the Internet for Additional Links

Enter in stock symbol: [   ] [Search] [Clear]

NOTE

This exceptional Web site—Wall Street Research Net—was found buried deep within a small business site. At the time, there were no other links found in business collections for this most useful business research site.

Business Directories and Collections

Listed below are online directories and collections of business resources.

- All Business Network (Fig. 5.31)
  http://www.all-biz.com

- Excite
  http://www.excite.com

- Galaxy
  http://galaxy.einet.net/galaxy.html

- Infoseek Guide
  http://guide.infoseek.com

- Madalyn
  http://www.udel.edu/alex/mba/main/netdir2.html

- GTE Supersite (Fig.5.29)
  http://superpages.gte.net

- I.O.M.A.
  http://www.ioma.com/ioma/direct.html

- Interesting Business Applications on the Net
  http://www.colorado.edu/infs/jcb/mbac6080/business.html

- Interesting Business Sites on the Web
  http://www.owi.com/netvalue/v1i1l1.html

- Net2 Business
  http://www.commerce.com/net2/business/business.html

- Yahoo
  http://www.yahoo.com

The GTE Superpages Interactive Services is another excellent business resource. There are two research services: Yellow Pages and Business Web Site Directory.

FIGURE 5.29
GTE Superpages—Yellow Pages

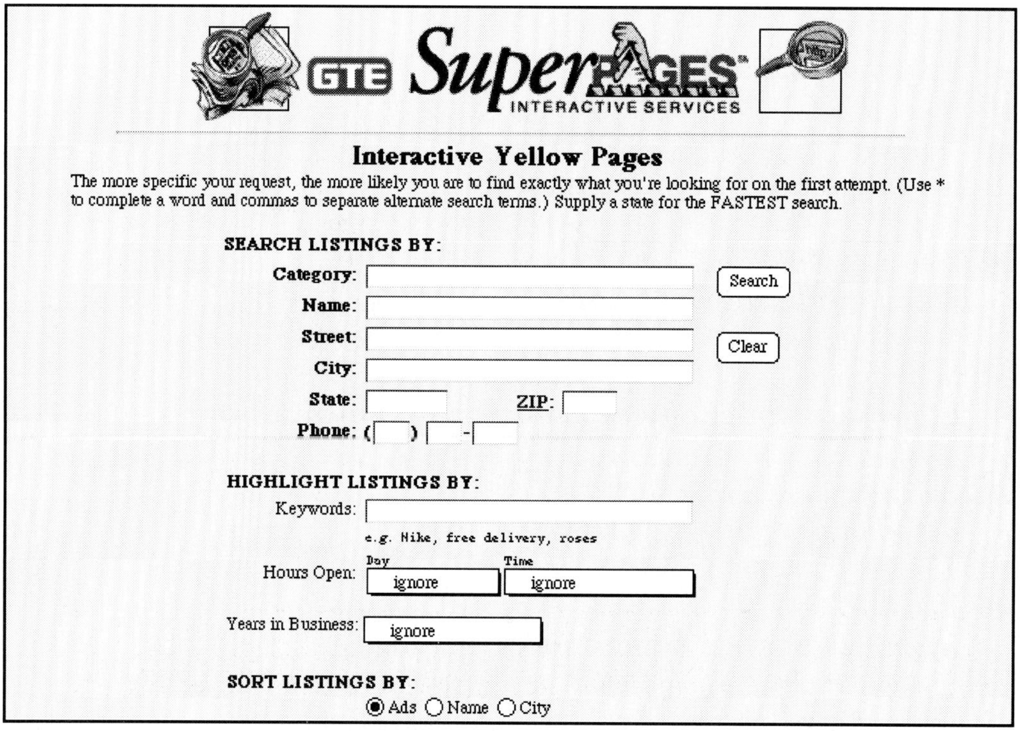

The Yellow Pages have a search tool to help you find comprehensive business information from over 11 million listings found in over 5,000 Yellow Pages directories from virtually every city in the United States. The Business Web Site Directory features links to over 60,000 business Web sites world wide.

FIGURE 5.30
GTE Supersite Business Web Site Directory

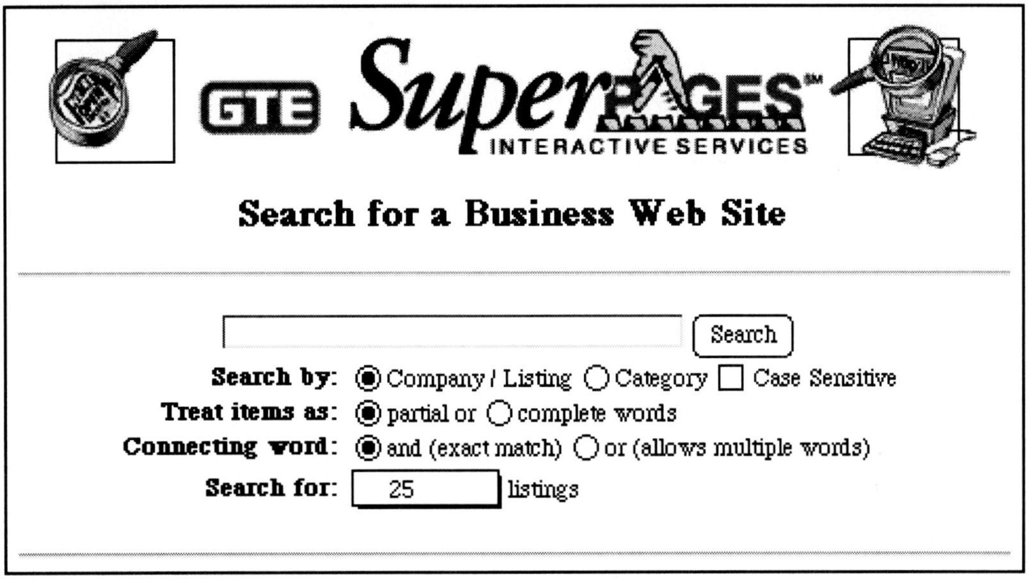

GTE Super**PAGES**
INTERACTIVE SERVICES

Search for a Business Web Site

[   ] [Search]

Search by: ⦿ Company / Listing ○ Category ☐ Case Sensitive
Treat items as: ⦿ partial or ○ complete words
Connecting word: ⦿ and (exact match) ○ or (allows multiple words)
Search for: [25] listings

The All Business Network site has a pull-down menu of business topics. Select a topic you are researching, and click the **Find It** button. You will then be given a list of descriptive links on the subject to explore.

FIGURE 5.31
All Business Network
Home Page

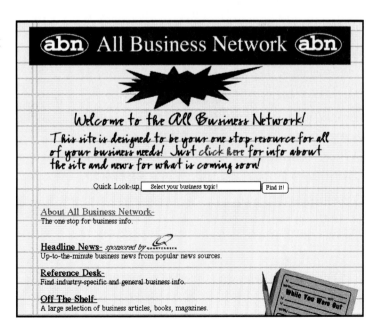

abn **All Business Network** abn

Welcome to the All Business Network!
This site is designed to be your one stop resource for all of your business needs! Just click here for info about the site and news for what is coming soon!

Quick Look-up [Select your business topic!] [Find it!]

About All Business Network-
The one stop for business info.

Headline News- *sponsored by* QUARTERDECK
Up-to-the-minute business news from popular news sources.

Reference Desk-
Find industry-specific and general business info.

Off The Shelf-
A large selection of business articles, books, magazines.

Links to Business on the Web

Listed below are links to national and multinational companies on the Internet.

- Commercial Sites Index
  http://www.directory.net

- HIP, HOT, 'N' HAPPENING
  http://pathfinder.com/@@7PcvogYAweyjsu6N/fortune/index.html

- Hot Business Sites
  http://www.hbs.harvard.edu/applegate/hot_business

- Interesting Business Sites on the Web
  http://www.owi.com/netvalue/v1i4l1.html

- Multinational companies on the Web
  http://web.idirect.com/~tiger/worldbea.htm

- The LIST
  http://www.sirius.com/~bam/jul.html

- The 25 Best Business Web Sites
  http://techweb.cmp.com:2090/techweb/ia/13issue/13topsites.html

- Web 100 Listing (Fortune 500 companies ranked by revenue)
  http://Fox.nstn.ca:80/~at_info/w100_uslist.html

- World Business on the WWWeb (a directory by business category)
  http://www.cba.uh.edu/ylowpges/ycategor.html

- Yahoo (Index to business on the World Wide Web—by category)
  http://www.yahoo.com/Business_and_Economy/Companies/Indices/

How to Reference Electronic Media

At the time of writing this guide, a standard had not yet emerged for referencing online information. As with any published reference, the goal of an electronic reference is to credit the author and to enable the reader to find the material. The International Standards Organization (ISO) continues to modify a uniform system of citing electronic documents. The following guidelines and examples have been compiled from *The American Psychological Association (APA) Publication Manual* and *The Chicago Manual of Style*.

- Be consistent in your references to online documentation or information.
- Capitalization follows the "accepted practice for the language or script in which the information is given."
- Use your discretion for the choice of punctuation used to separate elements and in the use of variations in typeface or underscoring to distinguish or highlight elements.
- If a print form is available and the same as the electronic form, referencing of the print form is preferred.

Include the following in your reference:

- The authors name if it is available or important for identification.
- The most recent date, if document undergoes revision.
- Title of the document, file, or World Wide Web site.
- Specify the protocol: Telnet, Gopher, FTP, World Wide Web.
- Provide the Internet address or retrieval path for accessing the information including the file name, directory, and pathway.
- Do not end a path statement with a period, because it is not part of the Internet address and may hinder retrieval if used.
- If the information is available via a listserv mailing list provide subscription information.

Format for Referencing Online Information

Author, I. (date). <u>Title of full work</u> [online]. Available: Specify protocol and path.

Author, I., & Author, I. (date). <u>Title of full work</u> [online]. Specify protocol and path.

Examples

World Wide Web

Riley, Margaret F. (1996). Employment Opportunities and Job Resources on the Internet [Online]. Available: http://www.jobtrak.com./jobguide

Gopher

Part I - M.U.S.E. Report (1993, December). [Online]. Available Gopher: gopher://naic.nasa.gov/   Pathway: /Guide to NASA Online Resources/ NASA Scientific, Educational, and Governmental Resources/ Government Resources/Americans Communicating Electronically/ Electronic Mail Issues for the Federal Government/ Unified Federal Government Electronic Mail Users Support Environment Report

File Transfer Protocol

"History and Philosophy of Project Gutenberg" (1992, August). In Gutenberg Archives [Online]. Available FTP: ftp://uiarchive.cso.uiuc.edu Directory: /pub/etext/gutenberg/history.gut

Listserv Mailing List

Smith, J., & Howell, A. (1995, December). "Effective Business Communication." In BUSCOM listserv archives [Online]. Subscribe: Available Listserv archive

---

NOTE

A Web site with information on the MLA style for documenting online resources is **http://www.cas.usf.edu/english/walker/mla.html**

CHAPTER 6
Gopher, FTP, and Telnet

• •

The World Wide Web is only a few years old—the first Web browser, Mosiac, was introduced in 1993. Prior to that time there was electronic mail, newsgroups, Telnet, FTP, and Gopher. Although the Web is the center of Net activity, there are many different and useful non-Web resources available. Before browers were available, access to these resources were done with software programs called *clients*. Today, all these resources can be accessed using your browser.

In this chapter you will learn how to use Netscape Navigator and/or Explorer to

➡ connect to Gopher servers to access information,
➡ explore FTP sites and transfer files (FTP) between two Internet sites, and
➡ access and communicate with remote computers using Telnet.

• •

Before You Begin...
Listed below are several points to remember as you begin your travels.

• The addressing information that defines the transfer protocols for accessing, viewing, and downloading information is different for each of these Internet navigational tools.

• When you access this information using Netscape or Explorer, remember that you are working within the World Wide Web environment. Information and access to files, data, and directories is by use of hyperlinks. Access these informational resources by clicking on the highlighted words.

• Navigate forward and backward using your browser's navigational tools: buttons and pull-down menus (including the history list).

- You can save bookmarks of your favorite places.

- Files that you download will automatically be saved on your hard drive.

- To travel outside the World Wide Web, just change the URL format.

For example,

This gopher address:	**cwis.usc.edu**
Becomes:	**gopher://cwis.usc.edu/**
This FTP address:	**ftp explorer.arc.nasa.gov**
Becomes:	**ftp://explorer.arc.nasa.gov**

Traveling Outside the Web—the URL

URLs are a standard for locating Internet documents. They are an addressing system for all Internet resources such as World Wide Web, Gopher menus, FTP file retrieval, Usenet newsgroups, and Telnet. Netscape uses the URL text to find a particular item among all the computers connected to the Internet. URLs specify three pieces of information needed to retrieve a document: the protocol to be used to transfer the information; the address of the server that stores the information; and the pathway to the information.

The format for a URL is **protocol://server-name/path**

Sample URLs

World Wide Web URL	http://home.netscape.com/index.html
Document from a secure Web server	https://netscape.com
Gopher URL:	gopher://umslvma.umsl.edu/Library
FTP URL:	ftp://ftp.netscape.com/pub/
Telnet URL:	telnet://geophys.washington.edu
Usenet URL:	news:rec.humor.funny

Gopher—Connecting to Gopher

Gopher is a navigational tool that uses a multi-level menu system to help find information and resources on the Internet. A *client* program is needed to access Gopher resources outside of the World Wide Web browser environment. Graphical software programs such as TurboGopher for the Macintosh and Gopher for Windows are most commonly used.

Notice the difference in how Gopher resources appear and are accessed via a non-graphical client versus a graphical browser such as Netscape Navigator or Explorer.

FIGURE 6.1
Gopher site without a graphical client

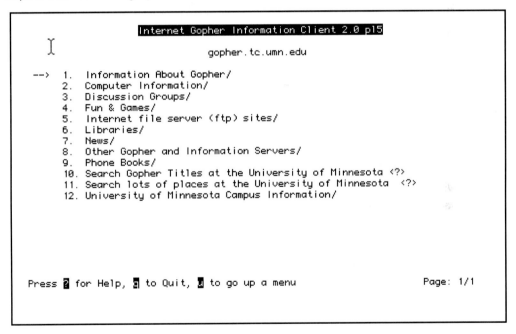

```
                      Internet Gopher Information Client 2.0 p15

   ⌶                        gopher.tc.umn.edu

   -->   1.  Information About Gopher/
         2.  Computer Information/
         3.  Discussion Groups/
         4.  Fun & Games/
         5.  Internet file server (ftp) sites/
         6.  Libraries/
         7.  News/
         8.  Other Gopher and Information Servers/
         9.  Phone Books/
        10.  Search Gopher Titles at the University of Minnesota <?>
        11.  Search lots of places at the University of Minnesota  <?>
        12.  University of Minnesota Campus Information/




   Press ? for Help, q to Quit, u to go up a menu          Page: 1/1
```

FIGURE 6.2

Gopher site with an Internet browser such as Netscape or Explorer

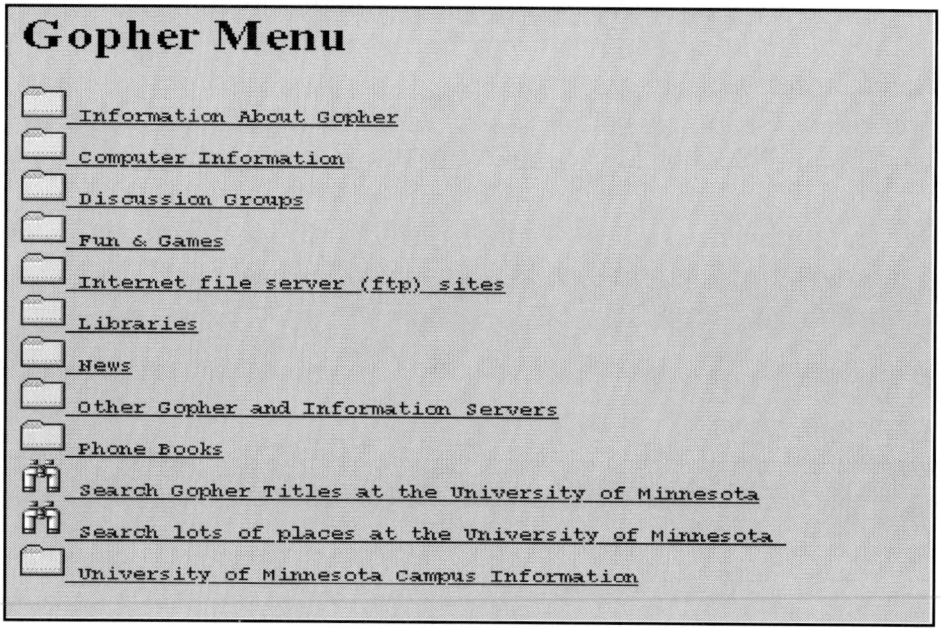

Gopher sites lack the rich formatting that you are accustomed to on the Web. Notice the menu is a list of hyperlinks. Each link is preceded by a small icon indicating the type of resource with which the link connects. Gopher links connect with

- menus
- text files
- images
- indexes
- movie and binary files

Gopher Addresses

Before you access information at a Gopher site, you need to know the Gopher address, which looks like this

gopher.tc.umn.edu or **cwis.usc.edu**

If you are accessing Gopher from an Internet shell account (text-based) or from a graphical client such as TurboGopher or Gopher for Windows, you type in an address such as **cwis.usc.edu** To use Netscape to access this same site, change the address to **gopher://cwis.usc.edu**

File Transfer Protocol (FTP)
Transferring Files With FTP

FTP is a special method used to transfer files between two Internet sites. Files or data can be sent to another site—uploading a file—or can be retrieved from a remote site—downloading a file. Many servers that make files available to Internet users are known as *anonymous* FTP sites. Any Internet user can log onto these sites and retrieve files. Before Web browsers, users would connect to an FTP site and login using *anonymous* as their username, and their e-mail address as their password. When using a Web browser such as Netscape or Explorer, this login procedure is taken care of by the browser software.

FTP resources contain computer software, databases, updates to most retail software, electronic texts, technical reports, journals, magazines, news summaries, books, images, and sound. One of the most widely used FTP services is to travel to FTP servers to download the most current versions of software such as Netscape, Explorer, Eudora, Helper Applications, or Plug-ins such as Shockwave and RealAudio. Using a browser to FTP makes file retrieval easy. Enter in the URL for the FTP site or the Web site that has a link to the FTP server, and just follow the links.

NOTE
One disadvantage of using a Web browser to access FTP sites is that the browser automatically logs you in as anonymous and uses your e-mail address as your password. Most FTP sites use this login for unregistered visitors. However, some FTP sites may require different login information. Consequently, you will need to use FTP software. Visit software sites such Jumbo (**http://www.jumbo.com**) and Tucows (**http://www.tucows.com**) for FTP software.

GUIDED TOUR...Traveling to an FTP Site

In this guided tour we will travel to the FTP site for Project Gutenberg. At this site you will find many archived books, including the classics. Type this URL in Netscape's **Location** field **ftp://uiarchive.cso.uiuc.edu**

FIGURE 6.3
Netscape link to the Gutenberg FTP site

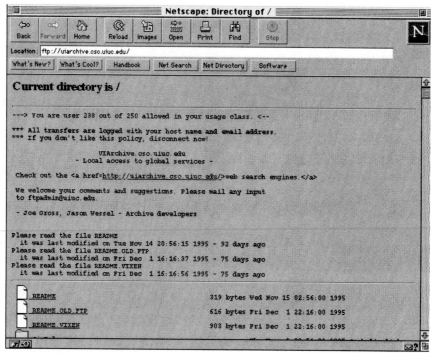

Notice that the FTP directory and content pages have minimal formatting. When possible, Netscape shows the type, size, date, and a short description of each file in a directory. The directory is presented as a list of links, each link preceded by a small icon indicating whether the link is a directory or a file. Clicking on a directory link brings you to another subdirectory.

Scroll down the list and notice the "README." files. These are text files with information about the FTP server. To read any of these text files, click once on the file's underlined name.

FIGURE 6.4
Hyperlinks to FTP resources using a browser

README 319 bytes Wed Nov 15 02:56:00 1995
README.OLD.FTP 616 bytes Fri Dec 1 22:16:00 1995
README.VIXEN 903 bytes Fri Dec 1 22:16:00 1995
SimTel Thu Nov 2 20:54:00 1995 Symbolic link
bin/ Tue Jun 6 00:00:00 1995 Directory
du.out 1573 Kb Tue Feb 13 18:45:00 1996
etc/ Tue Jun 6 00:00:00 1995 Directory
index.html Sun Oct 15 16:25:00 1995 Symbolic link
licensed/ Sun Dec 31 18:37:00 1995 Directory
local/ Thu Nov 23 02:11:00 1995 Directory
ls-lR.Z 3606 Kb Tue Feb 13 18:23:00 1996
pub/ Tue Feb 13 15:25:00 1996 Directory
usage.stats/ Fri Feb 2 20:18:00 1996 Directory
usr/ Tue Jun 6 00:00:00 1995 Directory

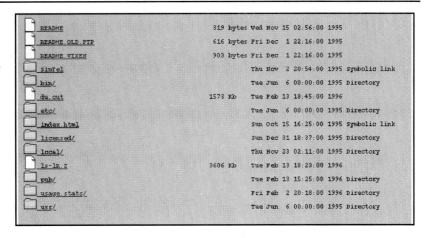

The icons that look like folders have an underlined name next to them followed by a slash (/). This indicates a link to a subdirectory. Follow this pathway to Project Gutenberg **/pub/etext/gutenberg** where each segment pub, etext, and gutenberg are displayed.

FIGURE 6.5
FTP directory for Project Gutenberg

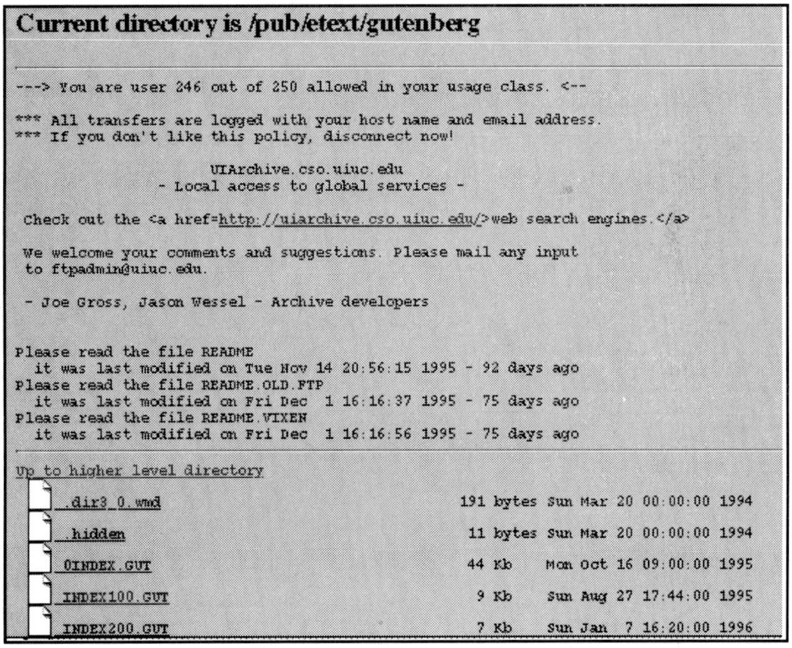

Current directory is /pub/etext/gutenberg
---> You are user 246 out of 250 allowed in your usage class. <--
*** All transfers are logged with your host name and email address.
*** If you don't like this policy, disconnect now!
UIArchive.cso.uiuc.edu
- Local access to global services -
Check out the <a href=http://uiarchive.cso.uiuc.edu/>web search engines.</a>
We welcome your comments and suggestions. Please mail any input
to ftpadmin@uiuc.edu.
- Joe Gross, Jason Wessel - Archive developers
Please read the file README
it was last modified on Tue Nov 14 20:56:15 1995 - 92 days ago
Please read the file README.OLD.FTP
it was last modified on Fri Dec 1 16:16:37 1995 - 75 days ago
Please read the file README.VIXEN
it was last modified on Fri Dec 1 16:16:56 1995 - 75 days ago
Up to higher level directory
.dir3_0.wmd 191 bytes Sun Mar 20 00:00:00 1994
.hidden 11 bytes Sun Mar 20 00:00:00 1994
0INDEX.GUT 44 Kb Mon Oct 16 09:00:00 1995
INDEX100.GUT 9 Kb Sun Aug 27 17:44:00 1995
INDEX200.GUT 7 Kb Sun Jan 7 16:20:00 1996

Notice the hyperlinks that access text files, software, images, and other subdirectories.

Before You Begin—Understanding Compression

Before you begin downloading files, it will be helpful to learn about compression. An important concept to understand is that any computer file that is going to be made available to other computers around the world needs to do two things.

- Be in a format that can be transmitted quickly from one computer to another.

- Be in a format that can be read by all computers (i.e., Macintosh, Windows, etc.).

To understand how this is accomplished you need to understand compression and helper applications because before you can view or use many multimedia files you may have to uncompress them and/or use a helper application to see or hear them.

Large files are compressed to save disk space and to make it faster to transmit them between computers. Software applications (that is, Internet browsers, Helper Applications, and compression programs) are examples of large files that you will be downloading to your computer from remote computers. More than likely these files will be compressed. Some of these files will be *self-extracting,* which means that the program will decompress by just double-clicking on it. If the file is not self-extracting, you will need a decompression program to open them. Likewise, if you are going to send large files, use a decompression program to make them smaller. Software applications are available to make your compressed files self-extracting.

The type of compression method used on a file is indicated by an extension added to the end of the filename. For example, many compressed Macintosh files end with **.sea.** A filename compressed using this method may look like this

Eudora2.1Fat.sea

Files ending in **.sea** are self-extracting archives and can be decompressed by double-clicking on the program icon.

Files compressed for the PC also have extensions to indicate the type of compression.

> **NOTE**
>
> Most decompression software programs can be downloaded from the Internet for free.

Macintosh Extensions and Compression

Macintosh compressed file extensions include

.cpt   A file compressed using CompactPro. CompactPro is a shareware program available on the Internet.

.hqx   A file compressed using the BinHex compression program. You must use BinHex, CompactPro, or Stuffit to decompress it.

.sea   A self-extracting archive. To open the file, double click on the file.

.sit   A file compressed using Stuffit. Use Stuffit Expander to decompress it.

.txt   An ASCII text file that can be read by virtually any computer using a simple text program.

One of the most commonly used decompression programs for Macintosh is Stuffit Expander. There are many Internet sites where you can find a copy of Stuffit Expander and download it to your computer by double-clicking on the Web link. After you obtain a copy of Stuffit Expander, place a copy on your desktop. When you receive files that need to be decompressed, drop them onto the Stuffit icon.

Two World Wide Web sites you can visit to search for compression software are JUMBO (**http://www.jumbo.com**) and Tucows (**http://www.tucows.com**).

The **All-In-One Search** page is another site to visit for links to freeware and shareware. **http://www.albany.net/allinone** When you connect to this page, scroll down and select the **Software** option.

PC Extensions and Compression

Some of the more common file extensions for the PC include

.asc   A simple ASCII text file that can be read by all computers.

.doc   A text file or a Microsoft word document.

.exe   A file that can be run by double-clicking on the file icon or from the Windows 95 Run command.

.zip   A file that has been compressed using the PKZIP compression program. To open or extract these files use PKUNZIP or WinZip.

The best Web site to find copies of compression/decompression software for the PC is TUCOWS—**http://www.tucows.com**. WinZip is frequently mentioned as the best for file compression/decompression. WinZip also makes an application for creating self-extracting archives.

Downloading Files

When files are downloaded to your computer, you are using FTP. FTP can be done in two ways

- enter in the FTP address for the FTP site
- go to a Web site that has links to FTP servers

In the following example we will visit a World Wide Web site with links to FTP servers for downloading the popular PC decompression program, WinZip.

1. Connect to the Internet.

2. Double-click on the Navigator or Explorer icon to launch the program.

3. Enter in the URL for the Web site—in this example, Tucows. Type Tucows's URL **http://www.tucows.com** in the Location field or click on the **Open** button. Hit Enter.

> ### NOTE
> If you are only looking for the WinZip utility, you may want to connect directly to their Web site at **http://www.winzip.com**

4. When you have connected to the software site, follow the links to the Windows utilities. You might want to take some time to look around at the other PC applications and utilities available from Tucows.

FIGURE 6.6
Tucows
Compression
Utilities
page

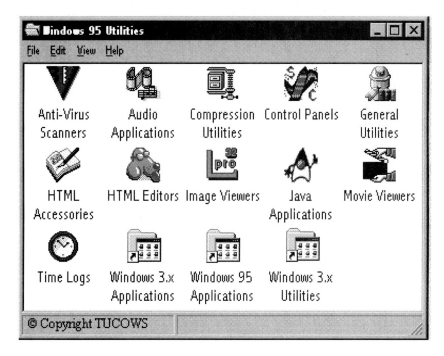

5. Click on the Compression Utilities link.

FIGURE 6.7

The Compression Utilities page for downloading compression software

6. Click on the WinZip for Windows 95 link.

> **NOTE**
>
> This example is for obtaining a copy of WinZip for Windows 95. If you are using Windows 3.1 follow the Tucows links to the Windows 3.1 page. If you are using a Macintosh, use the same procedure, but connect to a site with Macintosh software listed on page 97.

After Netscape makes contact with the remote FTP site, you will be asked for a location to download the file to. Select a location on your hard drive, then click the **Save** button. The file will now begin to download to the designated location on your computer. As the file downloads you will see a dialog box showing the status and progress of the file transfer.

Helper Applications for Viewing Images

Graphics images can be saved in as many as 50 different formats. These formats are merely different ways to preserve images. However, you will find that most images have one of these extensions **GIF, JPEG, XBM**.

GIF (Graphics Interchange Format) was created by CompuServe; JPEG (Joint Photographic Experts Group) is named for the group that invented it; XBM refers to X Bit Map format. Regardless of the format, images can only be seen by using an image viewer. Netscape Navigator and Explorer have the built-in capability to view images saved in these formats. You can also use these browsers to view images when you download them to your computer's hard drive.

Two popular image viewers for the Macintosh are GIFConverter and JPEGView. Obtain copies of these applications by visiting Jumbo and All-In-One sites. There are several image viewing programs for the PC: LVview Pro, Paint Shop Pro, Thumbs Plus, and VuePrint, and WebImage. Visit the TUCOWS Web for your PC viewers.

To see a listing of helper applications required to view image, video, and sound files, go Netscape's **Option** menu, select **General Preferences** and open the panel for **Helpers**. Find the name of the helper application for viewing the desired multimedia file.

Helper Applications for Sound & Video Files

Movie viewers allow users to view and manipulate movie files such as Quicktime or MPEG. Several of the more popular movie players for the PC are QuickTime Player, VMPEG Lite, and MPEG Movie Player. QuickTime is the most widely used movie player for the Macintosh.

Many sound files are heard using RealAudio. RealAudio makes it possible to hear sound immediately after clicking on a sound link. There is little or no time used to download the sound file. Visit the Web site **http://www.realaudio.com** for a copy of RealAudio. Visit the National Public Radio site **http://www.npr.org** to experience RealAudio.

Telnet

Telnet is one of the oldest Internet tools that allows users to log onto another computer and run resident programs. Although Telnet is not as visually interesting as the World Wide Web, it is essential to Internet travel. Telnet is a text-based environment requiring commands to navigate. Some Telnet access sites automatically link you to Web pages. Many Telnet sites, such as libraries, allow anyone to login without having a special account. Others require users to have a valid account before accessing many of the resident programs. Basic instructions for using telnet can be found at these Web sites

http://www.w3.org/hypertext/WWW/FAQ/Bootstrap.html
http://www.web.com. com/~futures/telnet.html

There are things you cannot do on the Web that Telnet can do better. For example, when you Telnet to a remote computer, frequently a mainframe supercomputer, you are working on another machine and are using that machine's speed and power. College students and business travelers dial a local Internet service provider and then Telnet to their college or business accounts to get their e-mail. Telnet saves them the cost of a long distance phone call.

Telnet also provides direct access to Internet services not always available from your Internet provider. Many of these services are exciting and interesting. Some open doors to alternative learning environments.

Some of the Internet services available using Telnet include

- databases (such as earthquake, weather, special collections)
- libraries (public, academic, medical, legal, and more)
- Free-Nets (noncommercial, community-based networks)
- interactive chats
- MOOs, MUDs
- bulletin boards

Databases

Many of the databases that you access with Telnet have the latest information on many topics like severe storms and weather conditions. Others, such as the Library of Congress, have archive collections.

Libraries

Telnet makes it possible to access libraries all around the world. Each library will vary on how much online help they make available to you.

Free-Nets

Free-nets provide networking services to a local community. Access to free-nets is achieved either at public libraries or by dialing in. To connect to a free-net, you will need to Telnet.

Free-nets establish their own resources for users in their community and are usually designed around a model of an electronic town. For example, you may be able to discuss local issues with the mayor or stop at an electronic school to discuss educational issues. These local networks usually have bulletin boards, electronic mail, informational resources, and educational resources. Educational resources may have local projects for classrooms or may provide information on national or international projects. Free-nets also provide links to global educational resources. They make finding and using Internet resources more manageable for educators who frequently do not have the time to explore cyberspace for classroom resources.

You may use a free-net as a guest, but your access privileges may be limited. You will have to register to have full access privileges. Registration is free to people within the community. For those outside the community, there is usually a nominal registration fee. Today, there are more than 30 free-nets online in cities across the United States and Canada. You can also find a few in Europe and New Zealand.

Chats

Chats are programs that allow you to talk to many people at the same time from all over the world. Internet Relay Chat (IRC) is the most widely used program. Many Internet access providers make IRC available to new subscribers. Some World Wide Web sites will have chat rooms for interactive discussion of topics of interest. For example, Time Warner's Pathfinder Web site has a chat room for discussing news of the day. Wired magazine has a chat room open for discussion. For more information on chats see Chapter 4.

MOO (*Multi-User Shell, Object Oriented*) and *MUD* (*Multi-User Domain*). MOOs and MUDs put visitors into a virtual space where they are able to navigate, communicate, and build virtual environments by using computer commands. Each of these environments uses a different type of software, but they are very similar in that users Telnet to a remote computer to create, communicate, and navigate in a text-based environment. Some MOOs and MUDs offer alternative learning environments such as Diversity University; others, fantasy role-playing games. New identities are created and experimented with. A popular Internet cartoon captures the essence of these virtual worlds and of the Internet when it shows one dog at a computer stating, "On the Internet, no one knows that you're a dog."

MOOs are very similar to MUDs, but use a more sophisticated programming language than MUD. A MOO lets users build things in a simulated environment by creating objects that are linked to a parent object. MUDs and MOOs are interactive systems suited to the construction of text-based adventure games and conferencing systems. The most common use, however, is multi-participant, virtual reality adventure games with players from all over the world.

Bulletin Boards
Usenet newsgroups are examples of bulletin boards (BBS). BBSs are places where people with similar interests can exchange information and share their thoughts with others without being logged on at the same time. Additionally, users can upload and download files and make announcements.

Telnet Software

Netscape and most browsers do not support Telnet. However, you can use Netscape to Telnet if you have a Telnet application program (a *client*) and tell Netscape where the program is located on your computer. When you type in a Telnet address, Netscape launches the application. When you are connected to the Telnet site, you will be in a text-based environment. There will not be hyperlinks for navigation. You will be using computer commands.

NOTE

Telnet programs are usually included with your TCP/IP software from your Internet provider. If you do not have a Telnet client program visit one of the Web software sites.

Configuring Netscape For Telnet

1. To find your Telnet client, open the Netscape application.

2. Go to the **Options** menu and select **General Preferences.**

3. Go to the **Applications** panel.

FIGURE 6.8
Netscape **Applications** panel

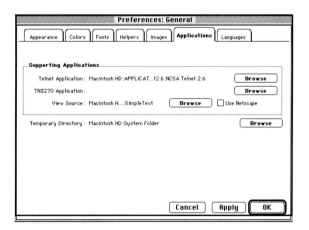

4. Click on the **Browse** button to find your Telnet client.

FIGURE 6.9
The **Browse** dialog box

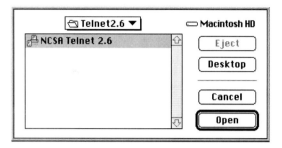

5. Click on the **Open** button. Netscape will now be able to launch the Telnet client program when you enter a Telnet URL.

GUIDED TOUR..Traveling to a Telnet Site

To visit a Telnet site using Netscape, type in the URL information. The format will be

telnet://address

We will now visit a Telnet site.

1. Type in this URL for the Smithsonian   **telnet://siris.si.edu**

FIGURE 6.10
Smithsonian
Welcome
screen

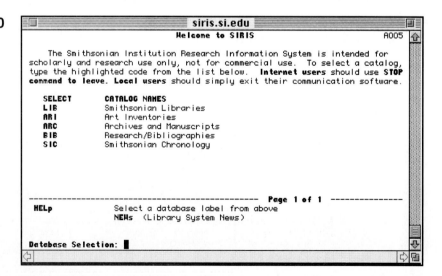

2. Select the Art Inventories Catalog and type in the code **ARI** next to Database Selection.

    Notice that you no longer have hyperlinks for navigation. Read all the information to find the command you must use for navigating at the site. This screen informs visitors to select the Smithsonian archive that they would like to visit.

FIGURE 6.11

Art Inventories Catalog, Smithsonian

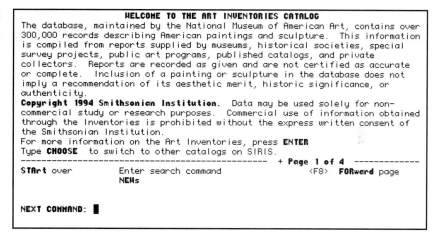

3. Read the Welcome screen for information on what command to enter to continue your exploration. In this case, we press the ENTER key.

FIGURE 6.12

The Art Inventories Catalog

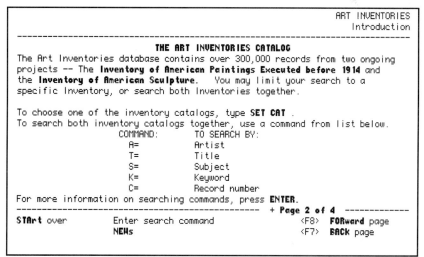

4. Search for information on Native Americans. The screen indicates to type in the command **K=name of keyword**. In this case we type *K=native americans*.

FIGURE 6.13

The result searching for *Native Americans*

```
Search Request: K=NATIVE AMERICANS                          ART INVENTORIES
Search Results: 23 Entries Found                            Keyword Index
---------------------------------------------------------------------------
      DATE  TITLE:                                       AUTHOR:
   1  1993  Touching Souls <3-dimen>                    Kaufman, Mico
   2  1992  Intersect <3-dimen>                         Canneto, Stephen
   3  1992  River Scenes at the Tennessee Aq <3-dimen>  Nivola, Claire
   4  1989  Buffalo Dance <3-dimen>                     Goodacre, Glenna
   5  1988  Maui Pohaku Loa <3-dimen>                   Toth, Peter
   6  1987  Prelude <3-dimen>                           Cunningham, Robert
   7  1985  The Immigrants <3-dimen>                    Hopen, W. D
   8  1985  The Future <3-dimen>                        Houser, Allan
   9  1982  Bodark Ark <3-dimen>                        Puryear, Martin
  10  1981  Trail of Tears <3-dimen>                    Toth, Peter
  11  1976  Native American <3-dimen>                   Toth, Peter
  12  1973  Cherokee Chieftain <3-dimen>                Toth, Peter
  13  1957  Ten O'Clock Line Monument <3-dimen>         Hollis, Frederick L
  14  1935  Hoover Dam Elevator Tower Relief <3-dimen>  Hansen, Oskar J. W
---------------------------------------------------- CONTINUED on next page ----
STArt over            Type number to display record        <F8>  FORward page
HELp                  MARK
OTHer options

NEXT COMMAND: █
```

5. To find information on the first title, type the number 1.

FIGURE 6.14

Information on *Touching Souls*

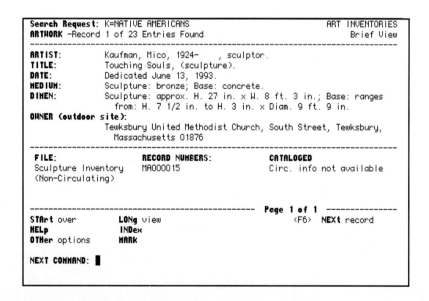

```
Search Request: K=NATIVE AMERICANS                          ART INVENTORIES
ARTWORK -Record 1 of 23 Entries Found                          Brief View
---------------------------------------------------------------------------
ARTIST:        Kaufman, Mico, 1924-    , sculptor.
TITLE:         Touching Souls, (sculpture).
DATE:          Dedicated June 13, 1993.
MEDIUM:        Sculpture: bronze; Base: concrete.
DIMEN:         Sculpture: approx. H. 27 in. x W. 8 ft. 3 in.; Base: ranges
               from: H. 7 1/2 in. to H. 3 in. x Diam. 9 ft. 9 in.
OWNER (outdoor site):
               Tewksbury United Methodist Church, South Street, Tewksbury,
               Massachusetts 01876
---------------------------------------------------------------------------
FILE:               RECORD NUMBERS:          CATALOGED
Sculpture Inventory MA000015                 Circ. info not available
(Non-Circulating)


--------------------------------------------------- Page 1 of 1 ---------------
STArt over        LONg view                        <F6>  NEXt record
HELp              INDex
OTHer options     MARK

NEXT COMMAND: █
```

Notice you can type *LONG* for a longer descriptive passage.

Gopher Resources for Business

Business Services on the Net Gopher
gopher://refmac.kent.edu
When you connect to this site, click on *Internet Resources Organized by Subject* for Total Quality Managment resources. Select the *Business Resources on the Net* link and you will connect to a Gopher page with business categories. Select a category and find information on valuable Internet sites.

Management Archive
gopher://ursus.jun.alaska.edu
The Management Archive Gopher server is an electronic forum for management ideas and information of all kinds. The Archive provides access to contributed working papers and preprints in the management and organizational sciences, course syllabi and teaching materials, archives of Academy of Management, and much more.

Simon Fraser University Gopher
gopher://hoshi.cic.sfu.ca
This Gopher is located at the Harbour Centre Campus of Simon Fraser University in Vancouver, Canada. It is a joint venture of the David See-Chai Lam Centre for International Communication and Management of Technology, both part of the Faculty of Communication at Simon Fraser University. This site is useful for the international business person.

University of California at Berkeley
gopher://infolib.lib.berkeley.edu
Select the link to *Research Databases* then *Business*. Here you will find the Berkeley Business Guide, and links to economic indicators and data, public policy, international business, management, industry information, electronic journals, and links to business and economic resources on the Internet.

Telnet Resources

Visit these Web sites for links to Telnet sites.
http://www.nova.edu/Inter-Links/start.html
http://www.magna.com.au/bdgtti/bdg_92.html#SEC95

Bulletin Boards

SBI Links to Bulletin Boards **http://dkeep.com/sbi.htm**
Guide To Select BBSs on the Internet **http://dkeep.com/sbi.htm**

Chats

WebChat Broadcasting System **http://wbs.net**
HotWired **http://www.hotwired.com**
The Palace **http:www.thepalace.com**
Globe **http://globe1.csuglab.cornell.edu/global/homepage.html**

Free-Nets

Community Computer Networks and Free-Nets
http://freenet.victoria.bc.ca/freenets.html

International Free-Net Community Listing
This page is a listing of Free-Nets and Community Nets around the world.
http://www.uwec.edu/Info/Freenets/

Gopher Links to Free-Nets
gopher://info.asu.edu:70/11/other/freenets

MOOs and MUDs

http://www.butterfly.net/~pyro/moo_page.html
http://www.bushnet.qld.edu.au/~jay/moo/
http://www.io.com/~combs/htmls/moo.html

Diversity University
http://www.academic.marist.edu/duwww.htm
telnet://moo.du.org:8888

Lambda MOO **telnet://lambda.parc.xerox.com:8888/**
HtMUD (a graphical MUD) **http://www.elf.com/~phi/htmud/**

PART II

The Web and Management

CHAPTER 7
Management Web Sites

• •

In this chapter, you will find many Internet resources to explore which help you discover how the Internet is being used in business and management. Additionally, you will learn how you can obtain the latest information on many management topics and issues. Categories include:

- Cool Business Web Sites
- Business Related Collections and Directories
- Business Resources—General
- Management and Organizational Behavior
- Entrepreneurship and Small Business
- Global Business
- Human Resource Management
- Management Listserv Mailing Lists
- Management Usenet Newsgroups

• •

Cool Business Web Sites

A cool site is hard to define—but you know it when you see it. This section explores cool Web sites, many of which have been given awards for excellence in content, design, and presentation. These sites are among the leaders creatively shaping the interactive media of tomorrow.

AT&T Business Network
http://www.bnet.att.com
This MUST VISIT site has links to many of the best busines resources on the Web as well as the latest business news and information.

AT&T Toll Free
http://www.tollfree.att.net/dir800
This Web site is one example of how a company has used the Internet to provide a useful service. The site helps you find 800 numbers of companies

nationwide. Shop for the things you need and want without ever leaving the comfort of your home anywhere in the United States.

Another site for finding 800 numbers is the **Internet 800 Directory**. **http://www.inter800.com/altindex.html**

Big Book
http://www.bigbook.com
VERY COOL SITE.... A MUST VISIT. Search for a U.S. company using the Big Book search engine. You will also be given an option to see a map of where the company is located. Store your favorite listings in a Personal Address Book. Be sure to explore their interactive map service. Enter in the street name, city, and state, and Big Book will generate a map for you. Big Book has street-level locations of 11 million U.S. businesses.

Business Management Home Page
http://www.lia.co.za/users/johannh/index.htm
This page is an entry point to all sources of information on the Web dealing with project management, total quality management (TQM), business process engineering (BPE) or reengineering (BPR), continuous improvement (CI), best manufacturing processes, benchmarking, productivity improvement, and related topics.

Digital Passport
http://www.rubicon.com/passport.html
This hot Web sit is worth a visit. Valuable and useful information is provided for those interested in international travel: an excellent world exchange rate tool, time zone information, international holidays, embassies, air travel information, and information on international deliveries.

Digital Planet
http://www.digiplanet.com/index.html
For anyone who wants to communicate a message, the most important issue is engaging and retaining one's audience. Whether conveying a corporate message or providing entertaining consumer content, Digital Planet explores the interactive medium's power to communicate a message that is entertaining, enlightening, and informative. Visit this site to learn how the Internet is being used to communicate with customers.

Diversity Resources
http://www.efn.org/~dennis_w/race.html
This award-winning web site is devoted to providing links to a wide variety of ethnocentric resources on the World Wide Web. An important site for learning more about diversity issues.

Fortune and CNN Financial
http://pathfinder.com/@@NAfrVQYAvuw7yzam/business
This page is a link from Time Warner's Pathfinder Web site. Explore the informative links from Fortune and learn more about business and business management. Explore CNN's Financial Network.

IDEAS—What a Great Idea!
http://redlt.com/idea
A MUST VISIT site. Have you ever had an idea and had it squelched? Or, have you ever killed someone else's idea? Visit this highly interactive and FUN site to learn about ideas. Take the Personal Killer Phrase Quiz and see if you are an idea killer.

Internet Plaza
http://plaza.xor.com
The Internet Plaza is an excellent place to begin when exploring online commerce. The Internet Plaza brings together exceptional Web sites for you to browse and enjoy. Explore virtual streets or proceed to the Plaza Town for an overview of everything the site has to offer.

National Public Radio
http://www.realaudio.com/contentp/npr.html
Stop by NPR online to see how audio is being used on the Internet. Visit the NPR archive to find your favorite programs.

Nijenrode Business
http://www.nijenrode.nl/resources/bus.html
This award-winning Web site focuses on resources relevant to students, faculty, and researchers at business schools.

PointCast Network
http://www.pointcast.com/products/index.html

Voted one of the best Internet applications, the PointCast Network (PCN) broadcasts news, financial news, stock quotes, weather, sports, and more to your desktop 24 hours a day. The PointCast Network is the first news network to use the Internet to broadcast news and information to a viewer's computer screen. The service is free, financed by advertising on the PointCast page. With "pointcasting" you can personalize the network to get just the news that interests you.

Another PointCast feature is PCN SmartScreen. Whenever your computer goes to sleep, the PCN SmartScreens (screen savers) kick in and display the latest news and information that PCN has delivered to you. You can even select the types of news and information you are interested in, from national and international news. Click on a headline in a SmartScreen, and the PCN Viewer displays the full text of that story.

FIGURE 7.1

PointCast page for viewing information on companies

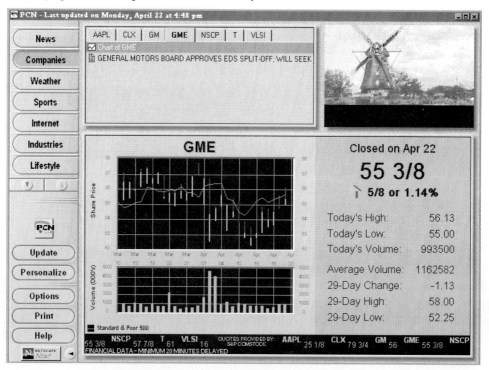

Sandbox
http://www.sandbox.net
Sandbox is entertainment with a clue—a free online network that explores how to use the Internet for entertainment.

Sea World/Busch Gardens—Anheuser-Busch
http://www.bev.net/education/SeaWorld
Visit this award-winning site and learn how a company provides useful and important services to the Internet community.

Switchboard
http://www.switchboard.com
Find friends, colleagues, and old roommates, or businesses. This service has over 90 million names with addresses, phone numbers, and personalized updates, and over 10 million businesses across the USA.

Violet
http://violet.com
Experience an entrepreneurial Internet venture by visiting Violet—a shopping boutique specializing in glorious luxuries, inspired necessities, and original gifts. Cross the threshold and be enchanted by objects with wit, personality, and style for your home, yourself, and your friends. **WARNING....** This site could be dangerous to addicted catalog shoppers.

Voyager
http://www.voyagerco.com
Visit this ever changing Voyager site to experience how one successful company uses art and technology.

Wall Street Research Net
http://www.wsrn.com
Wall Street Research Net consists of over 110,000 links to help professional and private investors perform fundamental research on actively traded companies and mutual funds, and locate important economic data that moves markets. A MUST VISIT site for those who want to find information on companies.

Business Related Collections and Directories

Listed in this section are Internet sites that will assist your business research and help you to locate online companies.

All Business Network
http://www.all-biz.com
This site would like to be your one-stop shopping site for business resources. A pull-down menu offers an excellent selection of business topics to connect to to find Internet resources. Winner of the "Top Business Site" award.

Commercial Sites Index
http://www.directory.net
The Commercial Sites Index lists businesses that have set up Home Pages on the Web. Make this a scheduled visit to see how companies are using the Net for business.

Galaxy
http://galaxy.einet.net/galaxy/Business-and-Commerce/Business-General-Resources.html
This search directory has links to business resources.

GTE Superpages
http://superpages.gte.net
This useful Web site will help you find information about businesses in their Yellow Pages or their Business Web Site Directory. In their nationwide Interactive Yellow Pages, you'll find comprehensive and accurate business information derived from over 11 million listings found in over 5,000 Yellow Pages directories from virtually every city in the United States. The Business Web Site Directory features links to over 60,000 Web sites owned and operated by businesses all over the world.

I.O.M.A
http://www.ioma.com/ioma/direct.html
Links to business resources including: financial management, legal resources, small business, human resources, and Internet marketing.

HIP, HOT, 'N' HAPPENING
http://pathfinder.com/@@7PcvogYAweyjsu6N/fortune/index.html
Fortune has identified 25 Very Cool Companies that are HIP, HOT, 'N'
HAPPENING. Visit this site to learn about "being cool on the Internet."

Hot Business Sites
http://www.hbs.harvard.edu/applegate/hot_business
Links to good examples of businesses using the Internet.

Institute of Management and Administration (IOMA)
http://www.ioma.com/ioma
Links to business resources.

Interesting Business Applications on the Net
http://www.colorado.edu/infs/jcb/mbac6080/business.html
Links to what business students at the University of Colorado believe to
be interesting uses of the Internet for business.

Interesting Business Sites on the Web
http://www.owi.com/netvalue/v1i1l1.html
Since its inception, the *Interesting Business Sites on the Web* page has
listed over 220 innovative and interesting sites for those interested in
business on the Net. Sites included are not just glitz, but appear to provide
a significant business value.

Madalyn
http://www.udel.edu/alex/mba/main/netdir2.html
Madalyn is an excellent starting place to explore business resources on
the Internet. Maintained by the University of Delaware MBA program,
this site has links to accounting, corporate information, economics,
entrepreneurship, ethics, finance, international business, management,
marketing, quality, and much more.

Net2 Business
http://www.commerce.com/net2/business/business.html
Links to business resources.

Small Business Resource Connections from IOMA
http://www.ioma.com/ioma/direct2.html#Small Business
Links to small business resources.

The LIST
http://www.sirius.com/~bam/jul.html
Links to businesses online.

Yahoo Business Page
http://www.yahoo.com/Business
Yahoo's links to business resources on the Internet.

Business Resources—General

This section introduces general Internet business sites to help you learn how companies are using the Internet for customer service, communication, information access, and dissemination.

AT&T
http://www.att.com/net
This AT&T site ranked 5th in "Best of the Best Business Sites."

Business Cartoons by Goff
http://www.fileshop.com/personal/tgoff/main.html
A Web site to capture a smile.

The Business of the Internet
http://www.rtd.com/people/rawn/business.html
An introduction to the Internet for commercial organizations with a focus on what the Internet can do for businesses: product analysis, market analysis, expert advice and help, recruitment of new employees, rapid information access, wide scale information dissemination, rapid communications, cost-effective document transfer, peer communications, and new business opportunities.

Business Netiquette International
http://www.wp.com/fredfish/Netiq.html

This rare and well done Netiquette resource provides useful information for business etiquette, with a focus on international business. You will also find links to other sites that offer Netiquette advice for personal communications.

CNN Financial Network
http://cnnfn.com/index.html
Links to business news including information on managing your money, managing your business, local and international business news.

Federal Express
http://www.fedex.com
FedEx provides a unique service from their site—tracking a FedEx package.

Glossary of Business Terms
http://cnnfn.com/resources/glossary/index.html
An excellent resource for finding the definition of business terms.

Harvard Business School Publishing
http://www.hbsp.harvard.edu
Resources and links to their products and services including the *Harvard Business Review*, *Management Update Newsletter*, *HBS Press and Reference*, and *Harvard Business School Cases*.

Hoover's Corporate Directory
http://cnnfn.com/resources/hoover/index.html
Search Hoover's Corporate Directory of over 10,000 public and private companies. Hoover's Master List Plus provides brief corporate profiles and links to company Web presence and other public information.

Internet Business Applications Guide
http://www.alter.net/busguide.htm
This site has links to a business guide for using the Internet to achieve a competitive business advantage.

Internet News Database
http://www.conceptone.com/netnews/netnews.htm
The Internet News Database is a free indexing and abstracting service

for the Internet community. Every day, they monitor the mainstream media and trade magazines for news related to the Internet and commercial online services. News is condensed into succinct summaries to give online entrepreneurs and marketers quick access to the information that most concerns them.

iWorld's Guide to Electronic Commerce
http://e-comm.iworld.com
This Web site provides comprehensive resources for commerce on the Internet. It has a list of links to sites designed to enhance commerce and trade using the instantaneous capability of online communications—from small business promotions to online banking to corporate advertising and government regulations.

MBA Page
http://www.cob.ohio-state.edu/dept/fin/mba.htm
Visit this site to find interesting Web resources of interest to business students. This page has been put together at Ohio State University with contributions from hundreds of people at schools around the world. It is designed to help MBA students survive and thrive.

MBA Student's Guide
http://www.cba.uga.edu/tcb/mbaguide/projweb.htm
The purpose of the online MBA Student's Guide is to help MBA students survive through the rigors of an MBA program.

MCI
http://www.internetmci.com
This site was voted one of the top business sites.

Pathfinder Business Resources
http://pathfinder.com/@@NAfrVQYAvuw7yzam/business
Pathfinder, an online service of Time Warner, has created an interesting Web page for Business and Finance.

Relais & Chateaux
http://www.integra.fr/relaischateaux
A well done Web site that provides links to worldwide resorts.

Seussville
http://www.seussville.com
Learn how Random House creatively markets their products at this interactive, fun site.

Seven Habits of Highly Offensive People
http://pathfinder.com/@@ymQGMAYAwOzAuISF/fortune/magazine/1995/951127/while.habits.html
Want to get ahead? Read this column by Stanley Bing from Fortune magazine.

Silicon Graphics
http://www.sgi.com
Surf this excellent site for a look at Silicon Graphics' products, services, and entertainment.

Sony
http://www.sony.com
The Sony site is an excellent example of how interactivity can be used on the Internet. It contains links to music, film, and electronics. Information can be found on musicians, their tour schedules, sound clips, record cover art, music videos, and special promotions, as well as information on Sony products.

Southwest Airlines
http://www.iflyswa.com
Visit Southwest Airlines' Home Gate for an example of interactive graphics.

Sun Microsystems
http://www.sun.com
Visit this Web site to learn more about a company that has focused on the convergence of the computer and communications industries.

United Parcel Service
http://www.ups.com
Learn more about how businesses provide useful services by visiting the United Parcel Service's interactive site. This site also helps you track

your packages, calculate approximate costs for sending a package, and a form to help estimate how long it will take for your package to reach its destination.

U.S. Chamber of Commerce and Business Development Organizations
http://www.commerce.com/net2/bin/travel/chamber.cgi
Links to U.S. Chambers of Commerce.

ZIP+4 Code Lookup
http://www.usps.gov/ncsc/lookups/lookup_zip+4.html
Have you ever been frustrated trying to find a zip code. This Web site by the United States Postal System provides a useful Internet resource. Enter an address; if found in their database, this interactive tool standardizes the address, returns the ZIP+4 Code, and provides the county name.

● ●

Financial Services

Fidelity Investment
http://www.fid-inv.com
Fidelity was one of the first financial services to establish a Web site believing that, given the right tools, individuals make their own best investment decisions. Their World Wide Web server provides investors with information and assistance to make more informed choices. It challenges visitors to find out how their personalities impact their ability to save. They can also check out how others scored on the same questions. The site also includes a contest and games.

Barrons Online
http://www.secapl.com/cgi-bin/qs
Free stock quote service.

Wall Street Interactive
http://wsj.com
Wall Street Interactive provides a continually updated view of business around the world. You'll find nearly every story from all the print editions of

the Journal, plus the Interactive Edition's own non-stop coverage and in-depth background. Features include links to additional information, such as the full text of documents or government reports mentioned in news articles, or expanded statistical information not found in the printed newspaper. A searchable archive of two weeks' worth of news from the Journal and Dow Jones news wires is also available.

Wall Street Research Net
http://www.wsrn.com
Wall Street Research Net consists of over 110,000 links to help professional and private investors perform fundamental research on actively traded companies and mutual funds and locate important economic data that moves markets. A MUST VISIT site for those who want to find information on companies.

● ●

Publishing / News
Web sites from publishing companies are excellent places to explore to learn how business is being transfored by the digital revolution.

Hot Wired
http://www.hotwired.com
Visit this innovative digital storefront that contains services, advertising, opportunities for advertising, special guest appearances, chat rooms, and much more. This site is an excellent example of the Internet's capabilities to deliver services and products.

NewsPage
http://www.newspage.com
NewsPage is one of the Web's leading sources of daily business news, with thousands of categorized news stories updated daily.

New York Times
http://nytimesfax.com/index.html
This site delivers highlights from the daily newspaper as well as articles on technology. You will need to download a copy of Adobe Acrobat reader (free) before you can read the *Times* online.

PointCast Network
http://www.pointcast.com/products/index.html
Voted one of the best Internet applications, the PointCast Network (PCN) broadcasts news, financial news, stock quotes, weather, sports, and more to your desktop 24 hours a day. The PointCast Network is the first news network to use the Internet to broadcast news and information to a viewer's computer screen.

San Jose "Mercury News"
http://www.sjmercury.com/main.htm
The Mercury Center Web is the first complete daily newspaper on the World Wide Web. This service offers continually updated news coverage, the complete text of each day's final edition of the *San Jose Mercury News*, including classified ads, and a variety of special features.

Time Warner
http://www.pathfinder.com
Pathfinder from Time Warner is an excellent Web site for discovering how an information-providing company pushes the capabilities of the new Internet medium.

The Wall Street Journal
http://www.wsj.com
This online version of *The Wall Street Journal* has hyperlinks to money and investing updates, a variety of *Journal* offerings including headlines from today's paper, and *The Wall Street Journal* Classroom Edition—the *Journal's* award winning educational program for secondary school students and teachers.

Wall Street News
http://wall-street-news.com/forecasts
Stop by WALL STREET - U.S.A. and drop in on the Internet Broadcasting Super-Station. Meet the News Director, Dr. Paul B. Farrell, who has a unique approach to financial news—the forecasting business. The news comes directly from financial newsletters published by Wall Street's leading forecasters. WSTN goes beyond just reporting the news, they forecast tomorrow's news today.

Management and Organizational Behavior

Basic Management Skills
http://www.ee.ed.ac.uk/~gerard/Management/index.html
At this site you will find a series of articles on basic management skills which appeared in IEE Engineering Management Journal: teams and groups, presentation skills, time management, quality in teams, writing skills, delegation, managing people, oral communication, project planning, and, becoming a great manager.

Benchmarking FAW Web Site
http://hpwww.epfl.ch/bench/bench.FAQ.html
At this Web site you will find many of the answers to benchmark questions derived from articles posted to the Usenet newsgroup, *comp.benchmarks*.

Visit this site for many links to benchmarking Web sites related to training, studies, articles, and publications.
http://www.apqc.org/b1/b1.htm

Business Management Home Page
http://www.lia.co.za/users/johannh/index.htm
This site deals with project management, total quality management (TQM), business process engineering (BPE) or reengineering (BPR), continuous improvement (CI), best manufacturing processes, benchmarking, productivity improvement and related topics.

Business Process Reengineering
http://ls0020.fee.uva.nl/bpr
Business reengineering is changing the organization and organizing the change.

Communications
http://www.smartbiz.com/sbs/cats/comm.htm
This Web site has links to many communication resources: business writing, telephone systems, employee communications, e-mail, presentations, mobile office, facsimiles, and much more.

Communication—The Internet a Revolution in Communication
http://www.nih.gov:80/dcrt/expo/talks/overview/index.html
This site has information on the Internet as a communication medium and links to information on the Internet revolution as reported in the media.

Communication Skills—Words of Mouth
http://www.cohums.ohio-state.edu/english/facstf/kol/diverse.htm
The Words of Mouth Home Page has been created to meet the needs of editors and others interested in learning more about communication skills.

Diversity Resources
http://www.efn.org/~dennis_w/race.html
This award-winning Web site is devoted to providing links to a wide variety of ethnocentric resources on the World Wide Web. Drop by this site to learn more about diversity issues.

• •

Creativity and Innovation

Creativity
http://www.ozemail.com.au/~caveman/Creative
Resources for creativity and innovation.

Visit this Web site for many links to wonderful creative resources on the Net. **http://www.ozemail.com.au/~caveman/Creative/cgroup8.htm**

IDEAS—What a Great Idea!
http://redlt.com/idea
A MUST VISIT site. Have you ever had an idea and had it squelched? Or, have you ever killed someone else's idea? Visit this highly interactive and FUN site to learn about ideas. Take the Personal Killer Phrase Quiz and see if you are an idea killer.

Mind Tools
http://www.mindtools.com
Mind Tools is a Web resource whose goal is to help you to optimize the

performance of your mind and achieve your dreams and ambitions. Take an online IQ test.

• •

Culture and Cultural Diversity

Afro America
http://www.afroam.org
Visit this well done Web site for information on African traditions, culture, and history.

Cultural Diversity
http://www.cohums.ohio-state.edu/english/facstf/kol/diverse.htm
Links to cultural diversity resources on the Internet.

Cultural Survival
http://www.cs.org
Cultural Survival, founded in 1972, helps indigenous peoples and ethnic groups deal as equals in their relations with national and international societies. Cultural differences are inherent in humanity and protecting this human diversity enriches our common earth.

Diversity Issues
http://www.shrm.org/docs/otherlnk.html#diversity
Links to Internet resources on diversity issues.

Diversity Database
http://www.inform.umd.edu:8080/EdRes/Topic/Diversity
The University of Maryland's diversity database contains local, national, and international academic material relating to the following areas of diversity as defined by the Office of Human Relations at the University of Maryland at College Park: age, class, disability, ethnicity, gender, national origin, race, religion, and sexual orientation.

Hispanic Pages on the Web
http://www.clark.net/pub/jgbustam/heritage/heritage.html
If you want to learn about the Hispanic culture begin at this well done Web site.

Indigenous Peoples of Mexico
http://web.maxwell.syr.edu/nativeweb/geography/latinam/mexico/
mex_main.html
Links to many resources to help you learn and better understand Mexico and the Mexican culture.

Native Web
http://web.maxwell.syr.edu/nativeweb
This award-winning site is a project of many people. Their vision touches ancient teachings and modern technology. Their purpose—to provide a cyber-place for Earth's indigenous peoples.

• • • • • • • • • • • • • • • • • • • •

Facilitation—Doing What Works
http://www.hursley.ibm.com/facer/facer.html
This IBM site looks at facilitation within organizations. You will also find links to information on organizational change.

The Keirsey Temperament Sorter
http://sunsite.unc.edu/personality/keirsey.html
The Keirsey Temperament Sorter by David Keirsey is a personality test which scores results according to the Meyers-Briggs system.

• • • • • • • • • • • • • • • • • • • •

Leadership

Bob Willard's Leadership and Management Development Page
http://www.oise.on.ca/~bwillard/leadaid.htm
Visit this page for many links to leadership and management development resources on the Internet.

Covey Leadership Center
http://www.imall.com/covey/covey.html
Australia: http://www.ozemail.com.au/~covey/
Stephen Covey believes that creating a personal mission statement is one of the most powerful and significant things you will ever do to take

leadership of your life. In response to overwhelming customer demand for additional help in creating personal mission statements, the Covey Leadership Center presents the CLC Online Mission Statement Builder. The Mission Statement Builder is a free service that will take between 10-15 minutes to complete. Visit the Covey Web site and create your mission statement. Explore their other resources.

Harrison on Leadership
http://www.altika.com/leadership
Harrison shares his thoughts on: leadership, character-based leadership, value-based leadership, servant leadership, corporate process reengineering, management for the 21st century, spirit in business, human and organizational behavior and responsibilities, technology and document management that facilitates leadership, and some words on motivation and success.

Leadership Management Development
http://www.oise.on.ca/~bwillard/leadaid.htm
This site has links to information to help facilitators of leadership/ management development.

Women and Leadership
http://www.cowan.edu.au/dvc/irwl/welcome.htm
The *International Review of Women and Leadership* is a journal published by Edith Cowan University which publishes articles, notes and reviews dealing with research findings, conceptual and theoretical developments, and commentaries on current practice in areas such as women's participation in various work and community environments, leadership styles and forms, cross-cultural aspects of women at work and in leadership positions, women in management, and education for leadership. At this site you will find abstracts of articles from past issues and links to other women's resources Web sites.

● ●

Learning Organization Online Dialog
http://world.std.com/~LO
A "Learning Organization" is one in which people at all levels, individually and collectively, are continually increasing their capacity to produce

results they really care about. This page has links to interactive discussions on learning organizations.

Management Archive
gopher://ursus.jun.alaska.edu
The management archive Gopher server is an electronic forum for management ideas and information of all kinds. The archive provides access to contributed working papers and preprints in the management and organizational sciences, course syllabi and teaching materials, archives of the Academy of Management and much more.

The management archive is an Internet information archive and server, using the Gopher system. They are currently undergoing major reconfiguration from a Gopher to a web site. Visit their Web site at **http://www.aom.pace.edu**

Managing in the Information Age
http://www.hbs.harvard.edu/applegate
Professor Lynda Applegate from Harvard Business School has created an interesting site for learning how to manage in the information age and how to do business on the Internet.

One World News Service
http://www.oneworld.org/news/news_top.html
Outstanding content with links to Internet resources related to human rights, ethnicity, and much more.

Operations Management
http://www.muohio.edu/~bjfinch/ominfo.html
This site is maintained by Byron J. Finch at Miami University (Ohio). It is designed to provide a starting point for accessing OM resources on the Internet. It contains links to a series of pages which are specific to OM topics, such as JIT, quality improvement, advanced technology, planning and scheduling, project management, operations research, productivity improvement, and others. It also contains links to numerous web search vehicles, some for general searches and some for searches of a more specific nature, such as Usenet, business sites, or government sites.

Prejudice
http://www.eburg.com/beyond.prejudice/Related.html
Links to Web sites related to prejudicial issues.

Project Management Forum
http://www.synapse.net/~loday/PMForum
The WWW Project Management Forum is a nonprofit resource dedicated to supporting development, international cooperation, promotion and support of a professional and worldwide project management discipline. You will find an interesting link to search tools to help find project management resources on the Internet. Additionally, there are links to project management resources, special interest sites, books, journals, magazines, and career search resources.

• •

Quality Resources

Business Management Home Page
http://www.lia.co.za/users/johannh/index.htm
This page is an entry point to all sources of information on the Web dealing with project management, total quality management (TQM), business process engineering (BPE) or reengineering (BPR), continuous improvement (CI), best manufacturing processes, benchmarking, productivity improvement, and related topics.

Quality Resources
http://users.aol.com/jaohunter/ongh.htm
This Web site has many links to online quality resources. A MUST VISIT site if you are interested in quality. One link connects you to an archive of over 700 articles on quality searchable by keyword.

System Dynamics Group—MIT
http://sysdyn.mit.edu/sd-group/home.html
The System Dynamics Group at MIT currently has three main areas of research: The National Model Project, The System Dynamics in Education Project, and the study of the Improvement Paradox—designing sustainable quality improvement programs. Visit their Web site to learn more about their research into decision policies in the National Model Project.

An NSF grant provides funding for the Improvement Paradox. Many firms abandon total quality programs due to lack of perceived impact on profitability, even after they experience a significant increase in performance. Through the development of formal models and original case histories, the Group seeks to identify the critical interactions between quality programs and other organizational structures. Visit their site to learn more.

● ●

Stress Links
http://www.ici.net/cust_pages/windy/stress.htm
We all know that stress maintains a firm hold on all of our lives in one way or another. However, how we let it control us is another story altogether. Visit this Web site and explore links to alternative methods of relieving stress.

Stress and You
http://www.mindtools.com/smpage.html
Articles at this site are written to help you understand how stress affects you, and explain a range of strategies and techniques that will help you control it. This review of stress management splits into three parts: understanding stress; finding your best level of stress; stress management techniques.

Stress Space
http://www.foobar.co.uk/users/umba/stress
At the Stress Space you will find information not found in conventional books—facts on stress and self-help information on how to manage it.

System Dynamics for Business Policy
http://web.mit.edu/15.874/www
Why do so many business strategies fail? System Dynamics for Business Policy uses a mixture of simulation models, role-playing games, and case studies to develop principles for successful management of complex strategies in a dynamic world. They consider strategic issues such as business cycles, market growth and stagnation, the diffusion of new

technologies, the misuse of forecasts, and the rationality of managerial decision making. Visit Professor Hines's Web site to learn more.

• •

Teams

Teams at IBM
http://www.hursley.ibm.com/facer/fac-docs.html
This Web site takes a look at teams at IBM. You will also find links to other related team documents.

Work Teams— Center for the Study of Work Teams
http://www.workteams.unt.edu
The Center for the Study of Work Teams is a non-profit organization created in 1991. Its vision is to become the premier center for research and education on collaborative work systems. You will find links to published research papers that cover a broad spectrum of topics within the general heading of "self directed work teams." You will also find many companies that work with work teams.

• •

Training and Development

TRAC
http://www.trainingaccesscenter.com
TRAC is an online commercial training resource center offering access to worldwide training and development resources. To learn about a free trial membership, visit their Web site.

Training and Development Via the Internet
http://cac.psu.edu/~cxl18/trdev
If you are interested in training and development, this is a MUST VISIT Web site. Dr. Ralph F. Wilson has provided many links to Internet resources of interest to trainers. Links to information and examples on using the Internet for training.

Training and Development Web
http://www.iconode.ca/trdev/t2.html
Links to many excellent training and development resources on the Internet.

●●●●●●●●●●●●●●●●●●●●●●●

Work and Family Issues
Dependent Care Connection
http://www.dcclifecare.com
The Dependent Care Connection® Inc. is the national leader in the delivery of child care and adult care counseling, education and referral. DCC programs and services establish "family friendly" work environments leading to decreased absenteeism, increased retention, enhanced recruitment, and overall productivity gains for the organization. For employees, DCC services lessen the time and stress associated with caring for loved ones and relieves the tension between home obligations and work responsibilities.

Family Network
http://families.com
Resources for the family, including information for the working family, educational issues, and a place to ask questions to the experts.

Labor Project for Working Families
http://violet.berkeley.edu/~iir/workfam/home.html
The Labor Project for Working Families was founded in September 1992 by a labor coalition. The Labor Project works with local unions to develop family policies at the workplace through collective bargaining. Work and family policies include family leave, flexible hours (part time, job share, flex time, telecommuting), child care and elder care benefits, sick time for families and domestic partner benefits. Visit their Web site to learn more.

Work and Family Issues Home Page
http://www.fsci.umn.edu/cyfc/work.htm
A MUST VISIT site from the University of Minnesota if you are interested in work and family issues. This excellent site has links to information on

these topics: work and family policies—a win-win formula for business and society; corporate values in a changing world; work and family dilemma; resources for family support; responsibility of business leaders to public education; United Way steps to success; meeting work and family challenge business perspective; working parent resource center, and more.

Entrepreneurship and Small Business

Advanced Business Consulting
http://www.webster.sk.ca/users/aic/abc.htm
This Web site has links to articles and Internet resources for entrepreneurs and small business owners.

Ask Mr. Equity
http://www.fegroup.com/mr_equity/index.html
Do you have questions about how to protect the equity in your franchise or how to increase your equity? Mr. Equity has the answers. Visit this Web site to find the answers or ask your own personal question.

AT&T Small Business Center
http://www.att.com/work/hoso.html
This site has information on how AT & T can help small business owners.

Best Businesses to Start in the 1990s
http://www20.mindlink.net/interweb/bestbusinesses.html
Have you been dreaming about your independence and can't stop thinking about the daily drudgery of the 6 a.m. shift or the hassle and boredom of the 9 to 5 routine? Visit this Web site to learn about the type of business that would best be suited to your particular needs. All businesses shown were especially selected on the basis of low start-up investment, high profit potential, and suitability to operate from home. Although you can view the 22 best businesses, there is a small fee to receive the report.

Business Information Resources
http://www.eotw.com/business_info.html
Links to magazines and journals, government and law, financial services and opportunities, regional and entrepreneurial organizations.

The Company Corporation
http://www.ibos.com/pub/ibos/company/home.html
Visit this Web site to learn how to form your own corporation by phone or by fax, in any state, in as little as 8 minutes, for as low as $45.

Copyright Home Page
http://www.benedict.com
This award-winning Web site has everything you will ever want to know about copyright.

Cyberpreneur's Guide to the Internet
http://asa.ugl.lib.umich.edu/chdocs/cyberpreneur/Cyber.html
The *Cyberpreneur's Guide to the Internet* is a guide to Internet-accessible resources of use to someone involved in entrepreneurial uses of the Internet, the *cyberpreneur*. This list was constructed as part of the class work for a course called Internet Resource Discovery, Organization, and Design, which is taught at the School of Information and Library Studies at the University of Michigan.

CyberPreneur
http://www.cyberpreneur.com
CyberPreneur—a very colorful and interesting Web site for small business owners and entrepreneurs. The goal of this site is to provide the latest news and the hottest opportunities available today, all with an Internet and small business focus.

Cultural Diversity
http://www.cohums.ohio-state.edu/english/facstf/kol/diverse.htm
Links to cultural diversity resources on the Internet.

DaVinci's Inventor Homepage
http://sulcus.berkeley.edu/Invention
This award winning site has invention and entrepreneurial information for the modern day Renaissance man or woman. A creative and informative Web site that should not be missed.

Deal Flow
http://www.dealflow.com

A virtual resource for accelerating deal exposure and evaluation in real-time.

Demographics—Internet
http://etrg.findsvp.com/features/newinet.html
http://WWW.Stars.com/Vlib/Misc/Statistics.html
http://www-personal.umich.edu/~sgupta/hermes/survey3
http://www.cc.gatech.edu/gvu/user_surveys
Learn more about Web visitors. Who are the users? What is their income level? Are they male or female? What are their buying patterns? What do they enjoy on the Web?

Doing Business on the Internet
http://www.smartbiz.com/sbs/dobiz.htm
This page contains links to resources to help you learn more about doing business on the Internet.

Also visit this site **http://netday.iworld.com/business** for an article by Robert Raisch on marketing a business on the global Internet.

EWEB — Resources for Entrepreneurship Education
http://www.slu.edu/eweb
EWEB's goal is to provide the best in one-stop-shopping for help in starting, running, and growing businesses—entrepreneurial firms, SMEs, small businesses, family businesses, home-based businesses, or new businesses. EWEB's target market is entrepreneurs, potential entrepreneurs (including students), and those who consult, or train, or educate entrepreneurs.

EGOPHER
http://www.slu.edu/eweb   Select the link to EGOPHER.
Last year, the entrepreneurship Gopher (EGOPHER) won a "Best of the INTERNET" award for its complete coverage of the field of entrepreneurship via the Net. EGOPHER has over 600 links, with about 100 based on the work of St. Louis University.

Entrepreneur's Corner Office
http://catalog.com/corner
If you have found this page for the first time, boy, are you in for a treat! If you're the non-traditional, non-conforming type that's always bucking the system, you're going to love this site! You're the one who's always asking "why not" when someone says "it can't be done." I'll even bet your favorite book is *If It Ain't Broke, Break It*, am I right?
—A Webpreneur

Entrepreneurial Edge
http://www.edgeonline.com
Visit this site to learn how to stay one click ahead of your competition.

Entrepreneur's Exchange Network
http://edgeonline.com/edge/market.htm
Exchange ideas, network, and mingle in this online networking forum. This forum provides a connection to others who provide a variety of services, information, and advice to keep you in touch and connected within your industry.

Entrepreneur Forum
http://upside.master.com/forum
Extensive resources for the entrepreneur—links to information on finance, consulting, advertising and public relations, recruitment, law. You will also find articles, a bulletin board for discussion, and Ask the Expert—a place to post a question to EF to answer.

Entrepreneur's Resources
http://www.catalog.com/intersof/commerce/entrepre.html
This excellent Web site has links to Web Resources for entrepreneurs, entrepreneurs' support organizations, businesses catering to entrepreneurs, and legal issues and resources.

Entrepreneur Resource Center
http://www.herring.com/erc
The virtual guide to financial and professional services (see Fig. 7.2).

FIGURE 7.2
Resources at the
Entrepreneur
Center

The Ultimate Guide to
Financial and Professional Services

Venture Capital

Investment Banks

Commercial Banks

Law Firms

Accounting Firms

Commercial Finance

Advertising Agencies

Executive Search

Economic Development

Entrepreneur/Small Business Newsletter
http://www.masterlink.com/masterlink/esbn
Each month The Entrepreneur/Small Business Newsletter has 5 feature articles on issues of interest to every small business. These feature articles are written by experts in their fields.

Family Business Center
http://199.103.128.199/fambiznc/cntprovs/orgs/necfb
This site is maintained by Northeastern University's Family Business Center. Visit this site to find information, articles, and newsletters to help family business owners manage their business's issues.

Idea Cafe
http://www.IdeaCafe.com
A cybercafe for entrepreneurs. Stop by for a chat.

Internet Invention Store
http://www.catalog.com/impulse/invent
An Internet business dedicated to showcasing new products and services.

141

Inventions and Patents
http://www.tucson.com/patents
Protect your idea before someone steals it. Visit this Web site to learn more.

Let's Talk Business Network (LTBN)
http://www.ltbn.com
A MUST VISIT site. The Let's Talk Business Network (LTBN) is a multimedia service driven organization focused on organizing, then uniting the extremely fragmented entrprepreneurial marketplace into a "one-stop entrepreneurial community." This interactive and entertaining playground of knowledge is the cornerstone of the Let's Talk Business Network "on-line." Visit the multi-purpose Entrepreneurial Center. Here you will find lots and lots of great audio clips, articles, FAQ's, "edutainment," and lots more. Its use of RealAudio for interviews with well-known entrepreneurs is what makes this a truly unique Web site for entrepreneurs and small business owners.

List Information Strategic Targeting
http://www.teleport.com/~list
The List Information Strategic Targeting site is for entrepreneurs looking for the best way to earn easy money from their own efforts. You will find useful links for transforming your efforts into success.

Microsoft Small Business Site
http://www.microsoft.com/smallbiz
Microsoft's small business site is definitely worth a visit. See how the technology wizards are using the Internet for business and, most importantly, for providing useful information to the small business owner. You will also find information on doing business on the Internet.

MIT Entrepreneurs Club (The MIT e-club)
http://www.mit.edu:8001/activities/e-club/e-club-home.html
The MIT Entrepreneurs Club (e-club) helps develop new business ventures. Their network was established to make the process of starting a business easier. The e-club includes MIT students, faculty, alumni/ae, friends, and professionals from outside MIT, representing a full spectrum of backgrounds in business, engineering, and the arts and sciences, including founders of innovative companies.

Net Marque
http://nmq.com

If you are interested in family business or putting your company in front of thousands of executives and owners of family-controlled firms, visit this site to learn more.

NOBO$$
http://www.noboss.com

This objective of NOBO$$, founded in 1978, is to enable you to search and evaluate an amazing variety of legitimate business opportunity sources that can be launched, established, owned and controlled with a capital investment under $5,000. Within these "Listings" you will find detailed information about scores of money-making enterprises ranging from chimney sweeping. . . to marketing on the Internet.

Patents
http://sunsite.unc.edu/patents/intropat.html

This is the home page for Source Translation and Optimization's (STO) Internet Patent Search System, a way for people around the world to perform patent searches and access information on the patenting process.

Price Waterhouse Venture Capital Survey
http://www.pw.com/vc

The Price Waterhouse Venture Capital Survey is a quarterly study of venture capital investments throughout the United States. The Price Waterhouse Survey Research Center contacts more than 1,000 venture capital firms to gather data on each firm's investments during the prior quarter. Visit their Web site to view the data results.

Resources for Entrepreneurs
http://www.DraperVC.com/Resources.html

Many excellent links to resources for entrepreneurs: job opportunities, government, industry, legal, people, and general resources.

Small and Home-Based Business Links
http://www.ro.com/small_business/homebased.html

This award-winning site is definitely worth a visit. You will find links to information on small and home based franchises, business opportunities,

143

small business reference material, information to help run and market your small or home based business, small and home based newsgroups, searching tools, services for small business, and much more.

SmallbizNet
http://www.lowe.org

SmallbizNet is an information toolbox for entrepreneurs, small business owners, and SOHO (small office/homebased office) workers. SmallbizNet is the Web's largest searchable full-text database for starting or operating your business. Open the lid on information services and sources that build your business.

Small Business Advancement National Center (University of Central Arkansas)
http://www.sbaer.uca.edu/homepage.html

SBANC is intended to help both entrepreneurs and entrepreneurship academics with the largest archive for the proceedings from academic conferences.

Small Business Advisor
http://www.isquare.com

Many excellent links to resources for small business owners and entrepreneurs. A MUST VISIT site.

Smart Business Supersite (SBS)
http://www.smartbiz.com

SBS was designed with one clear mission: to be the single most important source of high-quality, "how-to" business information on the Net.

U.S. Small Business Administration
http://www.sbaonline.sba.gov

SBA Online provides a wealth of information for small businesses and entrepreneurs. You will find information on starting, financing, and expanding your business. Explore their Great Business Hot Links or create a virtual business card. Links are also available to shareware for running a business. Virtually all SBA pamphlets are available for downloading 24-hours a day.

Small Business Center—Bell Atlantic
http://www.bell-atl.com/sbs
A well done commercial site that is worth a visit. See how the Internet is being used to provide SERVICE first in an interesting virtual environment.

Small Business Innovative Research
http://www.dsu.edu:8000
Between now and the year 2000 federal agencies managing the Small Business Innovation Research(SBIR) Program will award between five and six billion dollars to small company winners in technology focused competitions. Visit their Web site to learn more about how to qualify for federal grants.

Solidly Successful Entrepreneurs
http://www.wyoming.com/~SolidSuccess
The owner-operators of successful independent businesses follow a different set of "rules" than those promoted by management gurus for the executives of large, stultifying corporate institutions. Management philosophies attuned to the unique needs and opportunities of small and mid-sized businesses must be followed if business owners are to take full advantage of their "smallness," and if solid success is to be the ultimate result. Solidly Successful Entrepreneurs provides a showcase for displaying the fundamental management philosophies used by exemplars in achieving solid business success.

Venture Information Network for Entrepreneurs
http://www.thevine.com
Learn about growing and becoming part of growing companies.

The Virtual Entrepreneur Home Page
http://emporium.turnpike.net:80/B/bizopp/index.html
The Virtual Entrepreneur is a Web site and e-zine (electronic magazine) dedicated to the online entrepreneurs. Whether you are already in business for yourself or just interested in exploring new opportunities, The Virtual Entrepreneur is a worthwhile stop during your Internet travels.

Women's Connection Online
http://bbai.onramp.net:80/wco
An excellent online resource for women in general, especially entrepreneurial women.

Women Incorporated
http://www.womenconnect.com/wco/womeninc.htm
Women Incorporated is a new and exciting national not-for-profit membership organization dedicated to improving the business environment for women, especially entrepreneurial women.

Yahoo—Small Business Information
http://www.yahoo.com/Business/Small_Business_Information
This Yahoo directory has many links of interest to small business owners.

Global Business

Association of International Business Leaders
http://www.utexas.edu/students/aibl/
The purpose of the Association of International Business Leaders is to create a base of support for students with an interest in international business and political affairs. Another primary goal is to provide students an opportunity to discuss their ideas, to gain an understanding of different cultures, and to build on the diversity offered through such friendships. If you are a student interested in international business, this is a MUST VISIT site. There are also many excellent links on this page for those interested in international business.

Barrons Online
http://www.secapl.com/cgi-bin/qs
Free stock quote service.

Business Cards Online
http://www.webcom.com/bizcards
Create a virtual business card and post it online for 90 days. Visit this site to learn more.

Business Netiquette International
http://www.wp.com/fredfish/Netiq.html
This site claims to be the Web's only "Netiquette" site for information on international business etiquette for company-to-company business.

Business Travel
http://www.biztravel.com/guide
Information for the business traveler. Features include: travel news—information about business travel; and, countries—reports from world travelers.

Business Travel Library
http://www.craighead.com/craighead
A MUST VISIT site if you are traveling abroad on business. Craighead's Business Travel Library page has a list of over 50 countries around the world. Click on any country to review valuable country-specific information for the international business traveler. The information for each country is excerpted from Craighead's Business Reports, comprehensive 40-60 page reports designed to assist the international business person in conducting business abroad.

China on the Web
http://www.china-on-web.com
Learn about China's imports/exports, real estate, investment, travel, services, or about the China Project—dedicated to the children in the distressed mountain areas, the teachers working hard, and all the people offering their love.

Company Listings
http://ciber.bus.msu.edu/busres/company.htm
This Web site—a link from the International Business Resources on the Web—has links to directories and Web sites to help you find information on international companies. Valuable information to help you learn about the top multinational companies. Select the link to Fortune 500 Companies and find information on the global 500 List, Fortune's definitive ranking of the world's biggest industrial and service corporations, the global 500 ranked by performance and within industries, and the global 500 ranked within countries.

Currency Exchange Rates
**http://www.yahoo.com/yahoo/Economy/Markets_and_Investments/
Currency_Exchange**
This Yahoo page links to many excellent Web resources for currency exchange information.

One of the best sites for world exchange rates is
http://www.rubicon.com/passport/currency/currency.htm

Cyber Cafes in Europe
http://www.xs4all.nl/~bertb/cybercaf.html
The Cyber Cafes has links to Cyber Cafes throughout Europe that have their own Home Pages on the Net. Just virtually walk into one of the Cyber Cafes in this list and check out the place. Probably one of the more interesting things is that you can send home and receive your e-mail.

Digital Passport
http://www.rubicon.com/passport.html
This COOL Web sit is worth a visit. Valuable and useful information is provided for those interested in international travel: an excellent world exchange rate tool, time zone information, international holidays, embassies, air travel info, and information on international deliveries.

Economic Data
http://rampages.onramp.net/~tradelaw/europebus.html
This site has links to economy data on many international countries.

Eurochambers
http://www1.usa1.com/~ibnet/eurocham.html
Links to Chambers of Commerce in Andorra, Austria, Baltic Sea Region, Belgian Chambers Index, Croatia, Estonia, Finland, France, Germany, Ireland, Italy, Latvia, Netherlands, Romania, Slovenia, Spain, Sweden, Swiss Chambers Index, Turkey, and the United Kingdom.

Europages
http://www.europages.com
Europages is a pan-European guide unique in Europe, a contact tool designed specifically to meet the needs of companies seeking to trade

148

beyond their national borders. The directory lists 150,000 companies from 25 countries: a selection made from the 20 million existing European companies of the most dynamic, in terms of products, services, and export performance. A network of over 50 sales representatives sells advertising throughout Europe and the world.

European Business Center
http://www.euromktg.com/euromktg/eurobus.html
Although European Web sites represent 23% of all sites worldwide, it is often rather difficult to locate European businesses on the Web, since U.S. search engines cater nearly exclusively to the English-speaking world. This resource provides links to interesting European business sites, especially those not written in English.

Federal Market Place
http://www.fedmarket.com
Federal procurement and acquisition procedures are demystified to assist businesses in winning federal contracts.

Foreign Exchange Rates
http://www.dna.lth.se/cgi-bin/kurt/rates
Select a country and have the exchange rate computed for you based on the selection of a second currency.

Government Resources
http://ciber.bus.msu.edu/busres/govrnmnt.htm
For up to the minute information on international governments, visit this Web site for valuable resource links.

An extensive list of government resources on the Internet can be found at this site **http://www.eff.org/govt.html**

Index of Business Topics
http://www1.usa1.com/~ibnet/iccindex.html
The International Chamber of Commerce covers a vast range of subjects of vital interest to companies engaged in international trade. Visit this Web site to find business topics.

International Business Directory
http://www.et.byu.edu/~eliasone/main.html

This site from BYU has several valuable resources for international business. The Business Directory has links to the following international business resources: country information, currency exchange, databases, government sources, finance, foreign language/dictionaries, international news magazines, law, markets, stock indexes, terminology, and links to other international business directories.

In the IBD Collection you will find research projects and papers applicable to international business. This collection creates an opportunity for graduate students, faculty, and professionals from all over the world to have their work exposed. The intent is to provide some excellent information to businesses around the globe.

International Business Kiosk
http://www.webcom.com/one/world

A most informative site for those conducting international business. You will find links to information on the following: car rentals, country and city background information, diplomatic and consular representations, foreign currency exchange rates, health and travel, hotels, maps, hotel and package delivery, tourism offices, travel agencies on the Web, translators and interpreters, visas, weather around the world, weight, measurement, and other conversions.

International Business List
http://www.ibc-inc.com/intllist.htm

This page has links to international business sites by country. A wonderful page to begin with when looking for country specific information.

International Business Resources on the Web
http://ciber.bus.msu.edu/busres.htm

A goldmine of links to international business resources. A MUST VISIT site. Be sure you have lots of time to explore. Bring your compass, it's easy to get lost.

International Chamber of Commerce
http://www1.usa1.com/~ibnet/icchp.html

This Home Page introduces you to the universe of the International Chamber of Commerce and its thousands of member companies and associations in more than 130 countries. If you are engaged in international trade, this is the Web site for you. Consult it regularly to keep up with developments on the global marketplace that affect your business.

International Financial Encyclopedia
http://www.euro.net/innovation/Finance_Base/Fin_encyc.html
A wonderful resource for finding terms and resources for international financing.

International Law Page
http://www.noord.bart.nl/~bethlehem/law.html
This page has many excellent links related to international law, international organizations, human rights, treaties, and much more.

International Trade Law
http://itl.irv.uit.no/trade_law
This page has links to information on treaties, laws, and major international trade agreements.

International Trade and Law Links
http://rampages.onramp.net/~tradelaw/ILinks2.html
This Web site has one of the most comprehensive lists of links to information on international law, trade, and business.

Legal Issues
http://www.usitc.gov/tr/LEGAL4.HTM
This site has links to business legal information.

Multinational Companies on the Net
http://web.idirect.com/~tiger/worldbea.htm
This MUST VISIT Web site has chosen 125 of what it believes are the best world class supersites of multinational companies. They have divided the companies into 4 groups: large multinational manufacturing, large multinational service, small and medium multinational, and trade service firms. This is an excellent starting place to learn about how globally active companies are using the World Wide Web to promote themselves.

NAFTA Resource Center
http://www.i-trade.com/dir05
Anything and everything you ever wanted to know about NAFTA.

Nijenrode Web Server
http://www.nijenrode.nl/nbr/int
This site has links to many excellent International Web and Gopher sites.

One World Plaza
http://www.wincorp.com:80/windata/index.html
This award-winning Web site is worth a visit. One-stop shopping for world-wide business connections.

REESWeb
http://www.pitt.edu:80/~cjp/rsecon.html
REESWeb is sponsored by the Center for Russian and East European Studies at the University of Pittsburgh. Their Web site has links to resources on Russia, Poland, and countries of Central and Eastern Europe. You will also find general business, economics and law resources of interest to all regions.

The Trading Floor
http://trading.wmw.com
Rated the best international trade Web site. The Trading Floor is the first real-time, continuous-stream, international trade commodity exchange. Offering online trading, confidential negotiations, customized market and contact research at no charge, private company rooms, a blackboard of fresh trade leads and inquiries, an information-rich trader directory, thousands of industrial and agricultural trade contacts, thousands of industrial and agricultural market reports, unique multimedia brochures and catalogues, and much more. The Trading Floor is the most comprehensive interactive trading facilitator available in the online world for firms involved in international trade.

Using a proprietary discussion technology, subscribers to The Trading Floor can correspond in a highly sophisticated real-time manner with other subscribed traders around the globe. The Trading Floor is one of the most powerful tool available to build and leverage global contacts.

Wall Street News
http://wall-street-news.com/forecasts
Stop by Wall Street U.S.A. and drop in on their Internet broadcasting super-station. Meet the news director, Dr. Paul B. Farrell, who has a unique approach to financial news—the forecasting business. Their news comes directly from financial newsletters published by Wall Street's leading forecasters. WSTN goes beyond just reporting the news, they forecast tomorrow's news today.

Wall Street Research Net
http://www.wsrn.com
Wall Street Research Net consists of over 110,000 links to help professional and private investors perform fundamental research on actively traded companies and mutual funds and locate important economic data that moves markets.

WebFlyer
http://www.webflyer.com
Before you fly you may want to explore this site made available by Frequent Flyer Services. Can't remember what airlines and what hotels partner together to increase your awards? It's in here. Need to see an expert's review of a program for a certain carrier? It's in here 24 hours a day, 7 days a week.

World Bank
http://www.worldBank.org
Learn more about the World Bank's global partnership for development by visiting their Home Page.

Worldclass Supersite
http://web.idirect.com/~tiger/supersit.htm
This site provides step-by-step commentary for 500 top business sites in 70 countries, chosen on the basis of usefulness to world commerce, timeliness, ease of use, and presentation. The Supersite has six sections: reference, news, learning, money, trade, and networking.

World Clock
http://www.stud.unit.no/USERBIN/steffent/verdensur.pl
This award-winning site has a listing of local times for 124 world locations.

World Exchange Rates
http://www.rubicon.com/passport/currency/currency.htm
A well done and MUST VISIT site if you are interested in world exchange rates.

World Index of Chambers of Commerce
http://www1.usa1.com/~ibnet/chamshp.html
For centuries, Chambers of Commerce have been actively developing commercial and industrial opportunities around the world. Today Chambers of Commerce are joined together in an international network as members of the Global Network of Chambers of Commerce. Today there are more than 725 live Chambers and Associations of Chambers. Visit this site to find those online.

World Trade Organization
http://www.unicc.org/wto/Welcome.html
The World Trade Organization (WTO), established on 1 January 1995, is the legal and institutional foundation of the multilateral trading system. It provides the principal contractual obligations determining how governments frame and implement domestic trade legislation and regulations. And it is the platform on which trade relations among countries evolve through collective debate, negotiation, and adjudication.

Human Resources Management

Affirmative Action Resources
http://www.webcom.com/~garnet/labor/aa_eeo.html
Links to Internet resources for affirmative action and equal employment opportunity.

All Business Network
http://www.all-biz.com
This site would like to be your one-stop shopping site for business resources. Select the link to Human Resources for links to articles, publications, and general resources. This site was awarded "Top Business Site."

Ask a Human Resource Question
http://www.all-biz.com/winning/postqna.htm
Ask your special human resource questions to Ethan Winning, a consultant since 1977. Winning was national personnel manager for Komatsu America and a VP of personnel for Wells Fargo Bank. Also check out a log of questions.

ASTD Home Page
http://www.astd.org
ASTD (American Society For Training And Development) has information on shifting paradigms from training to performance. You will also find other useful freebies at their site.

Benefits Link
http://www.magicnet.net/benefits
This site has links to information and services for employers sponsoring employee benefit plans (including pension and profit-sharing plans), companies providing products and services for employee benefit plans, and individuals participating in employee benefit plans.

Big Dog's Human Resource Development Page
http://www.nwlink.com/~donclark/hrd.html
Need some information on training? Then visit this AMAZING online information resource. Here you will find a complete reference to implementing a system type training program. Included is information on the analysis, design, development, implementation, and evaluation.

Bureau of Labor Statistics
http://stats.bls.gov
One excellent feature of this site that adds to its value is the search tool to help you find information. You will also find links to helpful data on setting salaries or tracking benefits, the economy, surveys, publications, regional information, and research papers.

Cornell University School of Industrial and Labor Relations
http://www.ilr.cornell.edu
A well done Web site with links to valuable information for HR

professionals and students. The purpose of this Web server is to provide information about the School of Industrial and Labor Relations at Cornell University and its library, and to disseminate information on all aspects of employer-employee relations and workplace issues. Visit the electronic bookshelf for the latest articles, documents, and government reports. Within days of the release of the Glass Ceiling Report, the entire document was available online with associated references.

Department of Labor
http://www.dol.gov
A valuable site with statistics, information, and news of interest to HR management.

Employee Relations Web Pick
http://www.webcom.com/~garnet/labor
Here are a few of the topics from this site: lawsuits you should know about, U.S. Supreme Court rulings on labor law issues, resources on the Americans with Disabilities Act (ADA), Affirmative Action/EEO resources, links of interest to lawyers, law students, and those involved in litigation.

Fidelity Investment's Workplace Savings
http://www.fidelityatwork.com
The Workplace Savings area of the Fidelity Online Investor Center is a large Web site dedicated to meeting the needs of the millions of people who are saving for their retirement through workplace plans such as 401(k)s, 403(b)s, and others. It offers a wide range of information and interactive tools that can help you plan for retirement and understand the full value of participating in your employer's retirement savings plan.

Job Analysis and Personality Research
http://harvey.psyc.vt.edu
This site maintained by Virginia Tech has links to documents and data dealing with job analysis and job classification and personality assessment techniques.

HR Cyberspace Top 20
http://www.shrm.org/cyberspace/top20.html
HR Cyberspace is a monthly column in Society for Human Resource

Management's *HR Magazine*, reviewing Internet resources of interest to HR professionals. After reviewing hundreds of Web pages, they select what they believe are 20 of the most valuable sites. A good way to keep up on the best HR resources on the Net.

HR LIVE
http://www.jwtworks.com/hrlive
An online digest of monthly HR news, tips, views, and trends.

Human Resources and Benefits
http://www.ioma.com/ioma/direct2.html#Human Resources and Benefits
Links to human resources and benefits sites.

Human Resources Management Basics
http://members.gnn.com/hrmbasics/index.htm
Information and links on the basics of human resource management.

Human Resource Management on the Internet
http://members.gnn.com/hrmbasics/hrinet.htm
A truly AWESOME site with a plethora of links to human resource management resources on the Internet.

Human Resource Professionals Gateway to the Internet
http://www.teleport.com/~erwilson
Most of the information linked through this site has been included to assist the HR Professional with their personal and professional development.

OSHA (U.S. Department of Occupational Health and Safety Administration)
http://www.osha.gov
Links to information on statistics and dates, OSHA documents, publications, programs and services, compliance assistance, technical information, safety and health Internet sites, government sites, free software such as Asbestos Advisor, and more.

Safety Online
http://www.safetyonline.net
A well-done site with links to information and HOT safety topics.

Social Security Online
http://www.ssa.gov
This Home Page for the Social Security Administration provides valuable online services such as an online application for new or replacement Social Security cards, a service to compute your own benefit estimate (The ANYPIA Program), 1996 benefit and tax changes, benefit information, guide for employers, legislation, rulings, and more.

Society for Human Resource Management (SHRM)
http://www.shrm.org
SHRM represents more than 70,000 professionals and students around the world providing its members with education and information services, conferences, publications, and more. A MUST VISIT site for HR professionals and students. Although some of resources are only available to members, select HR in Cyberspace and find links to valuable information.

Top 25 Job Recruitment Web Sites
http://www.interbiznet.com/ibn/top25.html
Over 500 Recruiting Web sites were evaluated and reviewed in detail. This site has links to what they believe are the Top 25.

Training Net
http://www.trainingnet.com
This commercial site has training and human resources links including articles on training, a search tool to help you find quotes, and a free newswire service.

Ultimate Employee Handbook
http://www.courttv.com/seminars/handbook
This site appears to have grown from a special workshop devoted to a discussion of what makes a good employee handbook. You will find cool links to valuable resources related to this topic.

Virtual Office for the Human Resource Professional
http://www.idirect.com/hroffice

Visit the Virtual Office dedicated to the needs of the Human Resources professional. This site has resources to help you find information on the Internet related to Human Resources, as well as providing a forum for learning and sharing your knowledge and experience with other professionals in your field. Before you can take full advantage of all the online resources, you must become a member. At this time, there is no charge for becoming a member.

• •

Work and Family Issues

Dependent Care Connection
http://www.dcclifecare.com

The Dependent Care Connection® Inc. is the national leader in the delivery of child care and adult care counseling, education, and referral. DCC programs and services establish "family friendly" work environments leading to decreased absenteeism, increased retention, enhanced recruitment and overall productivity gains for the organization. For employees, DCC services lessen the time and stress associated with caring for loved ones and relieves the tension between home obligations and work responsibilities.

Family Network
http://families.com

Resources for the family, including information for the working family, educational issues, and a place to ask questions to the experts.

Labor Project for Working Families
http://violet.berkeley.edu/~iir/workfam/home.html

The Labor Project for Working Families was founded in September 1992 by a labor coalition. The Labor Project works with local unions to develop family policies at the workplace through collective bargaining. Work and family policies include family leave, flexible hours (part time, job share, flex time, telecommuting), child care and elder care benefits, sick time for families and domestic partner benefits.

Work and Family Issues Home Page
http://www.fsci.umn.edu/cyfc/work.htm
A MUST VISIT site from the University of Minnesota if you are interested in work and family issues. This excellent site has links to information on these topics: work and family policies—a win-win formula for business and society; corporate values in a changing world; work and family dilemma; resources for family support; responsibility of business leaders to public education; United Way steps to success; meeting work and family challenge business perspective; working parent resource center, and more.

• •

Job and Career Resources

America's Job Bank
http://www.ajb.dni.us/index.html
This online employment service offers information on over 250,000 employment opportunities.

Best Bets for Extending Your Search: Other Internet Job Guides
http://www.lib.umich.edu/chdocs/employment
This guide pulls together the Net's best sources of job openings and career development information, along with a description and evaluation of each resource.

CareerMosaic
http://www.careermosaic.com
Begin your CareerMosaic tour by visiting the J.O.B.S. database, with thousands of up-to-date opportunities from hundreds of employers.

Career Path
http://www.careerpath.com
Review employment opportunities from a number of the nation's leading daily newspapers such as *The New York Times, Los Angeles Times, The Boston Globe, Chicago Tribune, San Jose Mercury News,* and *The Washington Post.*

Career Resources Home Page
http://www.rpi.edu/dept/cdc/homepage.html

This Web site has links to online employment services including professional and university-based services.

CareerWeb
http://www.cweb.com
Search by job, location, employment, or keyword to find the perfect job. You can also browse employer profiles and search the library's list of related publications.

Employment Opportunities and Job Resources on the Internet
http://www.jobtrak.com/jobguide
Margaret F. Riley's Web site has excellent job resources. A MUST VISIT Internet stop.

E-Span
http://www.espan.com
E-Span, one of the countries foremost online recruitment services, provides tools designed to meet the needs of an increasingly competitive career market. Recently added to their services is Résumé ProKeyword Database that is available to more than 60,000 individually registered career service consumers. Visit this Web site and select Job Tools.

JobHunt
http://rescomp.stanford.edu/jobs
An award-winning Web site with a meta-list of online job-search resources and services.

Job Search and Employment Opportunities
http://asa.ugl.lib.umich.edu/chdocs/employment
Phil Ray and Brad Taylor, University of Michigan, present, best bets from the Net.

The Monster Board
http://www.monster.com/home.html
This unusual ad agency is a service for recruitment and furnishes information for job-seekers. A MUST VISIT site.

Stanford University
http://rescomp.stanford.edu

Stanford University's site provides listings of online job services such as Medsearch and the Chronicle of Higher Education. They also have links to other agencies.

Survival Guide for College Graduates
http://lattanze.loyola.edu/MonGen/home.html

This award-winning Web site has valuable information for college graduates seeking employment.

YAHOO Employment Resources
http://www.yahoo.com/Business_and_Economy/Employment

Links to employment resources on the Net.

■ ■

Communication Resources—Management Listserv Mailing Lists

Communite with others in the management community by subscribing to listserv mailing lists on topics of interest.

Important Information Before You Begin

Mailing lists have two different addresses.

1. An *administrative address* that you will use when you

   - subscribe to the list
   - unsubscribe from the list
   - request information or help

2. A *submission address* used to send your messages to the list.

The Administrative Mail Address

Most listserv mailing lists use software such as listserv, majordomo, or listproc that automatically processes users' requests to subscribe or unsubscribe. Some examples of administrative addresses used for subscribing and unsubscribing are:

listserv@uga.cc.uga.edu
majordomo@gsn.org
listproc@educom.unc.edu

NOTE

Requests for subscriptions are usually processed by computers, therefore, type the commands without any changes. Be sure to enter the exact address that you have received, duplicating spacing and upper-and lowercase letters. Do not add any other information in the body of your message. If your e-mail package adds a signature, be sure to take it off before sending your request.

After you join a listserv mailing list, you will usually receive notification of your subscription request and an electronic welcome. This message will provide you with information such as the purpose of the list, the names of the listserv's owners, how to subscribe and unsubscribe, and other commands to use for the list.

> ## NOTE
> Save a copy of this listserv welcome message. Later you may want to refer to it for information on how to unsubscribe or perform other operations related to the list.

The Submission Mail Address

Mail sent to the submission address is read by all of the subscribers to the list. This address will be different and should not be used for communicating with the list administrator. Here is an example of an address for sending your messages to the mailing list participants:

itforum@uga.cc.uga.edu

For this mailing list, the first word is the name of the list, *itforum* (instructional technology forum). Any mail sent to this address will be sent to all subscribers to the list. This is the address used to communicate with subscribers to the list.

• •

Subscribing to a Listserv Mailing List

In this section you will find a list of management listserv mailing lists. You will be given the address to which to send your request and the subscription request format for the BODY of your message (see Fig. 7.1). Leave the SUBJECT field blank. If your e-mail program requires you to make an entry in the SUBJECT field, insert a period (.).

The format for each listserv will be the same as in the example (Fig. 6.1).
ADDICT-L

> Address: listserv@kentvm.kent.edu
> Subject: leave blank
> Body: subscribe ADDICT-L <firstname lastname>

FIGURE 7.1
Subscription to a listserv showing the administrative address and the subscribe command

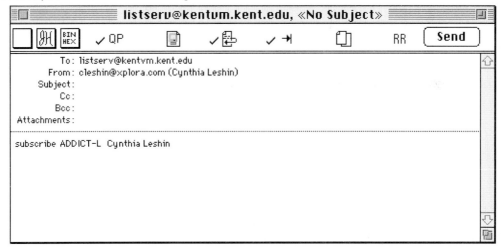

Before You Begin...

read *Tips for New Users of Listservs and Newsgroups* on page 214.

BizCom (Business communication research, pedagogy, and practice)
Address: listproc@ebbs.english.vt.edu
Body: subscribe BizCom <firstname lastname>

BSN-D (Business Sources on the Net—Distribution List)
Address: listserv@listserv.kent.edu
Body: sub BSN-D <firstname lastname>

BTECH94 (Business Technology)
Address: listserv@umslvma.umsl.edu
Body: sub BTECH94 <firstname lastname>

Business Management

BPR-L (Business Process Reengineering)
Address: listserv@is.twi.tudelft.nl
Body: sub BPR-l

BPR-L (Business Process Reengineering)
Address: mailbase@mailbase.ac.uk
Body: join BPR

CHANGE (initiating and sustaining major change in organizations)
Address: majordomo@mindspring.com
Body: info change

CQEN (Community Quality Electronic Network)
Address: tom.glenn@tqm.permanet.org
Body: join CQEN

CQI-L (Continuous Quality Improvement) (moderated)
Address: listserv@mr.net
Body: subscribe CQI-L

DEMING ELECTRONIC NETWORK (moderated)
Address: den_moderator@a1.rscc.cc.tn.us
Body: join DEN

DIVERSITY-FORUM (issues related to diversity, not limited
solely to, but including the world of work)
Address: majordomo@igc.apc.org
Body: subscribe diversity-forum

Downsizing
Address: majordomo@quality.org
Body: subscribe downsizing

ISO 9000 (Quality Standards; moderated)
Address: listserv@vm1.nodak.edu
Body: subscribe ISO9000

LDRSHP (for the exchange of ideas about all aspects of leadership)
Address: LISTSERV@iubvm.ucs.indiana.edu
Body: SUB LDRSHP <firstname lastname>

Learning Organizations (very active)
Address: majordomo@world.std.com
Body line 1: info learning-org
Body line 2: end

PM-NET (The Project Management mailing list)
Address: pmnet-request@uts.edu.au
Body: subscribe PM-NET

TQM (Measurement of Product and Service Quality)
Address: tqm@cua.cameron.edu
Body: subscribe TQM

Quality (moderated and very active)
Address: listserv@pucc.princeton.edu
Body: Subscribe Quality

Quality Management (based in the UK)
Address: mailbase@mailbase.ac.uk
Body: join quality-management

REGO-QUAL (Creating Quality Leadership and Management)
Address: Listproc@gmu.edu
Body: subscribe REGO-QUAL

REGO-ORG (Transforming Organizational Structures)
Address: Listproc@gmu.edu
Body: subscribe REGO-ORG

TEAMNET-L (work team research topics; devoted to research)
Address: roquemor@terrill.unt.edu
Body: subscribe teamnet-l

TQM-D (an unmoderated version of the previous quality list; active list)
Address: majordomo@quality.org
Body: subscribe tqm-d

TQM-L (Total Quality Management in Higher Education)
Address: listserv@ukanvm.bitnet
Body: subscribe TQM-l

TQMEDU-L (educational issues)
Address: listserv@humber.bitnet
Body: subscribe TQMEDU-l

For quality-related lists visit this Web page: **http://www.quality.org/ qc/html/emailing.html**

WARIA-L (Workflow And Reengineering International Association)
Address: majordomo@quality.org
Body: subscribe waria-l

• • • • • • • • • • • • • • • • • • • •

Training and Development
See this Web site: **http://www.iconode.ca/trdev/t5.html**

• • • • • • • • • • • • • • • • • • • •

Entrepreneur—Small Business
HomeBased-L (discusses non-Internet and Internet sales and marketing strategies for home-based businesses and or entrepreneurs)
Address: listserv@Citadel.Net
Body: SUBSCRIBE HomeBased-L

IMARCOM (issues related to marketing on the globalIinternet)
Address: IMARCOM@INTERNET.COM
Body: SUBSCRIBE IMARCOM your name, company name

Let's Talk Business Mailing List (for entrepreneurs and small business owners) Visit their Web site to signup online.
http://www.ltbn.com/listform.html

MIT e-club (a list to keep interested people up-to-date on MIT's entrepreneurial work)
Address: e-club-request@mit.edu stating
Body: Tell who you are and a brief background on your interests.

To learn more, visit their Web site and signup online.
http://www.mit.edu:8001/activities/e-club/emaillist.html

NetMarket-L (for entrepreneurs, webmasters and business people who are testing out ideas and marketing concepts on the Internet)
Address: listserv@Citadel.Net
Body: NetMarket-L

YELLOWPAGES (discussion and education of the small business person regarding advertising on the Internet)
Address: yellowpages-request@webcom.com.
Body: subscribe yellowpages <firstname lastname>

● ● ● ● ● ● ● ● ● ● ● ● ● ● ● ● ● ● ● ●

Global Business

Ginlist - Global Interact Network (discussion of international business and marketing issues by business professionals worldwide)
Address: listserv@msu.edu
Body: SUBSCRIBE GINLIST <firstname lastname>

Busfac-L (International Business Faculty Discussion)
Address: listserv@cmuvm.csv.cmich.edu
Body: SUBSCRIBE BUSFAC-L

GlobMkt (applied global marketing
Address: listserv@lsv.uky.edu
Body: SUBSCRIBE GLOBMKT

International Business Discussion Group (discussions by international business owners, government trade officials, international consultants, and trade desk)
Address: woolford@trip.net
Subject   SUBSCRIBE INTL. BUSINESS
Body: your company name and address, email, URL, and
              short description of products and services

Tbirds (forum to discuss the challenges of international business, plus job and resource announcements)
Address   listserv@listserv.arizona.edu
Body: SUBSCRIBE TBIRDS

TRADE (discussions of international trade policy)
Address: listserv@csf.colorado.edu
Body: SUBSCRIBE TRADE

Trade (a daily publication devoted to the worldwide distribution of commercial advertising for businesses engaged in the wholesale buying/selling of large lot merchandise and commodities internationally)
Address   trade-l-request@intl-trade.com
Subject: SUBSCRIBE
Body: SUBSCRIBE

TradeCom (promotes commercial contacts)
Address: TradeCom-request@bigdipper.umd.edu
Body: SUBSCRIBE

Trade-News (Trade News mailing list provides two separate weekly bulletins: Trade Week in Review and NAFTA Monitor)
Address: kmander@igc.apc.org
Body: SUBSCRIBE TRADE-NEWS <your e-mail address>

Mavenconference (for people who want in-depth discussions of marketing and sales related issues relative to their work. Mavenconference provides access to a group of seven internationally known marketing consultants who answers subscribers' questions)

Address: listserv@mail.telmar.com
Body   SUBSCRIBE MAVENCONFERENCE <firstname lastname>

CET On-Line (news service intended for those interested in business in Central and Eastern Europe)
Address   cet-online-request@eunet.cz
Body: SUBSCRIBE

China-Link Import/Export News (international business in China and the Pacific Rim)
Address: listserv@ifcss.org
Body: SUBSCRIBE CHINA-LINK <firstname lastname>

Eeurope-Business (exchange of business leads in former Eastern Europe)
Address: listmanager@hookup.net
Body: SUBSCRIBE EEUROPE-BUSINESS

EUMEDNET (promotion of the use of the Internet among the small and medium enterprises in the European and Mediterranean countries)
Address: listserv@listserv.rediris.es
Body: SUBSCRIBE EUMEDNET <firstname lastname>

• • • • • • • • • • • • • • • • • • • •

Human Resource Management
ADA-LAW (legal aspects of ADA)
Address: listserv@ndsuvml.bitnet
Body: subscribe ada-law <firstname lastname>

BENEFITS-L (issues related to employee benefits)
Address: listserv@frank@mtsu.edu
Body: subscribe benefits-l <firstname lastname>

BPR   (issues related to business process reengineering)
Address: mailbase@mailbase.ac.uk
Body: join bpr <firstname lastname>

CARDEVNET (career development issues)
Address: cardevnet-request@world.std.com
Body: subscribe end

DIVERSITY-FORUM (issues related to diversity, not limited
solely to, but including the world of work)
Address: majordomo@igc.apc.org
Body: subscribe diversity-forum

Futurework (issues related to the future of work)
Address: listserv@csf.colorado.edu
Body: subscribe futurework <firstname lastname>

H-Labor (issues related to labor history)
Address: listserv@uicvm.uic.edu
Body: subscribe h-labor <firstname lastname>

HRIS-L (issues related to the changing nature of information systems
in HR and payroll)
Address: listserv@yorku.ca
Body: subscribe hris-l <firstname lastname>

HRNET (general HR issues)
Address: listserv@cornell.edu
Body: subscribe hrnet <firstname lastname>

HR-OD-L (Human Resource and Organizational Development and
Change Network)
Address: listserv@ksuvm.ksu.edu
Body: subscribe hr-od-l <firstname lastname>

IERN-L (industrial relations and HRM issues)
Address: listserv@ube.ubalt.edu
Body: subscribe iern-l firstname lastname

IOOB-L iIndustrial psychology discussion group)
Address: listserv@uga.cc.uga.edu
Body: subscribe ioob-l <firstname lastname>

JOBANALYSIS (job analysis discussion list)
Address: listserv@listserv.vt.edu
Body: subscribe jobanalysis firstname lastname

Learning-Org (issues related to systems thinking and the learning organization)
Address: majordomo@world.std.com
Body: subscribe learning-org <firstname lastname>

MGTDEV-L (management and executive development issues)
Address: listserv@miamiu.muohio.edu
Body: subscribe mgtdev-l <firstname lastname>

NWAC-L (issues related to the changing nature of work)
Address: listserv@psuvm.psu.edu
Body: subscribe nwac-l <firstname lastname>

ODCNET-L (issues related to organizational development)
Address: listserv@psuvm.psu.edu
Body: subscribe odcnet-l <firstname lastname>

PAYHR-L (issues relating to payroll and HR)
Address: listserv@vm1.ucc.okstate.edu
Body: subscribe payhr-l <firstname lastname>

TRDEV-L (training and development issues—very active list)
Address: Listserv@psuvm.psu.edu
Body: subscribe trdev-l <firstname lastname>

Communication Resources – Management Usenet Newsgroups

> **NOTE**
> The ClariNet Hierarchy is a different type of newsgroup in that it is a read-only group. It is like a newswire service that has pre-selected articles relating to one subject area. Not all Internet sites have ClariNet since there is a charge at the institution level for receiving it.

alt.business.multi-level - multi-level (network) marketing businesses
alt.business.seminars - business seminars
bit.listserv.buslib-l - business libraries list
bit.listserv.e-europe - Eastern Europe business network
bit.listserv.japan - Japanese business and economics network.
clari.biz.briefs - business newsbriefs
clari.biz.earnings - businesses' earnings, profits, losses
clari.biz.features - business feature stories
clari.biz.industry.health - the health care business
clari.biz.misc - other business news
clari.biz.misc.releases - releases on general business topics
clari.biz.top - high-priority business news
clari.usa.gov.policy.biz - U.S. business and economic policy
misc.business.facilitators - forum for group facilitation professionals
misc.business.marketing.moderated - roundtable for marketing topics

Global Business

alt.business.import-export - business aspects of international trade.
biz.marketplace.international
biz.marketplace.international.discussion

Entrepreneur–Small Business

alt.business.import-export
misc.business.consulting - the business of consulting
misc.entrepreneurs - discussion on operating a business
misc.entrepreneurs.moderated - entrepreneur/business topics

CHAPTER 8
LEARNING ADVENTURES
MANAGEMENT

● ●

This chapter provides activities to facilitate learning how to use the Internet as a valuable tool in management.

➮ Traveling in Cyberspace
➮ Managers and Management
➮ Entrepreneurship and Small Business Management
➮ Global Business

● ●

Traveling in Cyberspace

What is the Internet?

1. Write a metaphor for the Internet.

2. Today there are between 30-50 million Internet users. How do you see the Internet impacting your life? Your career?

3. Being on the Internet means having full access to all Internet services: electronic mail, Telnet, File Transfer Protocol (FTP), and the World Wide Web. Make a map that illustrates your understanding of what it means to be connected to the Internet.

4. Visit these Web sites using either Netscape Navigator or Microsoft Internet Explorer. Make bookmarks of sites you would like to save.
   http://espnet.sportzone.com
   http://mosaic.larc.nasa.gov/nasaonline/nasaonline.html
   http://www.cybertown.com
   http://www.kbt.com/gc
   http://www.microsoft.com
   http://www.paris.org

5. Organize your bookmarks by categories by creating file folders.

6. Export your bookmarks to a floppy disk.

7. How do you think that the Internet will be used in the future? For business? For personal use? In the field of management?

8. Design a personal Home Page that provides information about yourself.

9. Is the Internet a useful tool or just a fun, new technology that produces the "Oh Wow . . . this is cool" experience?

Chatting on the Net

1. Visit these Web sites and search for a listserv in your field of study.
    http://www.tile.net/tile/listserv/index.html
    http://liszt.com

2. Subscribe to several listserv mailing lists.

3. Use Netscape to explore Usenet newsgroups. Look for 5-10 groups related to your field of study.

    Visit this Web site for a listing of Usenet newsgroups.
    http://ibd.ar.com/ger

    Visit this Web site and use a simple search tool to locate Usnet newsgroups of interest.
    http://www.cen.uiuc.edu/cgi-bin/find-news

4. Visit these Web sites to experience Internet chat.
    WebChat Broadcast System **http://wbs.net**
    HotWired **http://www.hotwired.com**
    The Palace **http:www.thepalace.comg**
    Globe **http://globe1.csuglab.cornell.edu/global/homepage.html**

5. Do you see a use for online chats for business in the future?

Finding Information and Resources

Select a topic of interest (i.e., a hobby, sport, country, a trip you plan to take, or a management issue).

1. Use Yahoo, Excite, Galaxy, and Magellan to research your topic. Begin by investigating their subject directories. After you have explored the directories, do a keyword search.

2. How do Yahoo, Excite, Galaxy, and Magellan differ in the way they provide access to information? Do you find one better or more useful than the other?

3. Explore the Advanced Options in Yahoo to refine and limit your search. Conduct a search using the Advanced Options. Did you get better returns?

4. Use each of the following search engines to research your topic: Excite, Alta Vista, Infoseek, and Open Text. Before you use these search engines, read how to use their advanced options for a more efficient search.

5. Compare and contrast Excite, Alta Vista, Infoseek, and Open Text. Which one did you find most useful in providing the information you were searching for? What are the advantages of each? Disadvantages?

6. How do search tools such as Yahoo and Magellan differ from search engines such as Excite, Alta Vista, Infoseek, and Open Text? Do you think there would be times you would find one more useful than another?

7. Begin a category or a file folder in your Internet browser for Internet research tools. Make bookmarks of search tools that you find helpful.

8. What does the future hold for Internet search tools?

Managers and Management

The Internet is a revolutionary new communication technology that is re-defining human communication, consumer behavior, and information sharing. Small businesses to large corporations are exploring this new medium, trying to better understand how to tap its potential for future success. The Internet is and will continue evolving and growing into an important resource for business. As a manager, it is essential that you understand the power and capabilities of the fastest growing communication media that we have ever experienced. Your future will inevitably include computer-based communication and information tools and resources. Strategic planning within organizations will need to take into account the power and capabilities of the Internet to provide information access and dissemination.

One way to begin to better understand the power of the Internet as a tool for business is to visit business World Wide Web sites and analyze how they are promoting their companies, communicating with customers, building relationships, sharing information, and perhaps most importantly, what the design elements are that attract customers and keep them returning. As you explore the Internet, you will also learn that the Net is a valuable resource for finding the latest and most current information on any topic of interest. Information is available on the Internet before it is available via the traditional print media.

1. Begin your learning adventure by visiting this Web site with links to the 100 biggest American corporations online. **http://fox.nstn.ca** Scroll down the page and click on Web 100. Or direct at **http://Fox.nstn.ca:80/~at_info**

   Write a paper in which you discuss the use of the Internet as a new technology for business. Topics for discussion include:

   - How are companies using the Internet to communicate with customers? What services are being provided to customers?

- How are companies using this new medium differently than traditional media to communicate?

- Do companies attempt to build a relationship with their customers? How?

- Do you think the medium is being used effectively to communicate?

- Why would a potential customer want to visit these sites?

- Which Web site is most impressive? Why?

- What makes the site friendly, informative, easy to navigate, and persuasive? What keeps this site from having these important features?

- Would a customer want to return to this site?

- Can you perceive a sense of the company's corporate culture through a visit to their Web site?

2. How can the Internet improve communication with customers?

3. Discuss how you have changed the way you communicate with others in the last 10 years. How do you prefer to communicate? How do you think a customer prefers to communicate?

4. Work in small groups and discuss how the Internet can open new markets for a business.

5. Visit **Interesting Business Sites on the Web** at this URL
   http://www.owi.com/netvalue/v1i1l1.html
   How do these online companies communicate a message? How do they engage their visitors? What service do they provide?

6. Define Internet communication.

7. The tools used for communicating with customers have changed dramatically in this decade. Prior to the 1980s communication was in person, by U.S. mail, or by telephone. In the 1980s new tools for one-to-one communication were introduced: express mail, fax, cellular phones, and computers. In the 1990s interactive communication such as computer networks, interactive television, videoconferencing, and the Internet have opened new doors to improve business-customer communication. Compare how products and services were delivered to customers prior to the 1980s, in the 1980s, are delivered in the 1990s, and will be delivered in the year 2000. Include in your discussion the advantages and/or disadvantages of communication tools of each of the four time periods.

8. How do you communicate with companies you buy products from? Describe good business-customer communication experiences you have had. Describe bad business-customer communication experiences. How does this effect your loyalty to the company? How does it effect your satisfaction with the product?

9. Why is Internet literacy important for managers?

10. Cyborganic is a new kind of business that is building a hybrid community space with online and offline components. Visit their site. Stimulate your mind. Create a new business using online and offline components. **http://www.bud.com**

11. Visit this Web site **http://www.wp.com/fredfish/Netiq.html** Use the resources from this site to write "Guidelines for Personal Communication Netiquette."

Managing in a Global Environment
12. Successful global management requires that managers become polycentric and develop an appreciation and enhanced sensitivity to differences in customs and practices of people from other countries. How can the Internet act as a tool for managers in this respect? Research Web sites to support your discussion.

13. How can the Internet help a company take advantage of the new global marketplace?

14. Research companies such as IBM (**http://www.ibm.com**), Ford (**http://www.ford.com**), and Bristol-Meyers Squibb (**http://www.bms.com**) that are moving to globalize their management structure. Do their Web sites provide information on their global organization? Do you perceive differences in how these companies are managed and operated based on their Internet information? Look for links to their mission statement, management resources, and global links. How do these sites differ? How are these companies using the Internet?

15. Visit Web sites of multinational corporations

Intel	**http://www.intel.com**
Toyota	**http://www.toyota.com**
Siemens	**http://www.siemens.de**
Sony	**http://www.music.sony.com/Music/MusicIndex.html**
Microsoft	**http://www.microsoft.com**
Apple	**http://www.apple.com**
Ford	**http://www.ford.com**
Coca Cola	**http://www.cocacola.com**
Chevron	**http://www.chevron.com**
XEROX	**http://www.xerox.com**

What do the Web sites tell you about the company's global connections?

16. Visit these Web sites and explore the online businesses. Many of them, such as Reebok, are about to go international. Learn more about how they are using the Internet for global marketing.
http://Fox.nstn.ca:80/~at_info
http://www.sirius.com/~bam/jul.html
http://www.directory.net/dir/directory.html

Social Responsibility and Values-Based Management
17. Ben & Jerry's Homemade Inc. is one example of a company that has

tried to invoke a sense of social responsibility. They purchase Brazil nuts, cashew nuts, and vanilla from rain forests. Clever naming of ice cream flavors—Rainforest Crunch, Peace Pops, Cherry Garcia— and creative flavor descriptions on the cartons cleverly reveal the company's commitment to social issues and causes. Visit their Web site (**http://www.benjerry.com/aboutbj.html**) and read their Statement of Mission.

How do you feel about this company's being socially responsible? Do you believe that this is just a marketing hook?

18. Use Ben & Jerry's Web site as a starting point to discuss how you feel about cause-related marketing. Is this just another profit-maximizing behavior? Visit other Web sites such as Reebok (**http://planetreebok.com**) and Ford (**http://www.ford.com**) to see how they differ in their corporate approach to cause-related marketing.

19. Select a business that you are interested in. How could *values-based management* be used to profit your company as well as genuinely support an important cause? As a starting point, research Web sites of companies that you are interested in to learn more about them.

Managing Your Career—Career Opportunities on the Internet
For the following activites, refer to the Web sites on pages 160-162.

20. The Internet is providing new opportunities for job-seekers and companies to find good employment matches. Many companies are turning to the Internet believing that the people who keep up with the most current information and technological advances in their fields are the best candidates for positions. The growing perception among employers is that they may be able to find better candidates if they search online. Visit the Web sites listed in Chapter 8 and review online résumés. Print examples of 5 different types of résumés that illustrate how the Internet is being used to showcase talents and skills. Be prepared to discuss online résumés in small groups.

21. In small groups discuss how the Internet changes the way résumés are designed, developed, and delivered. How does the Internet put you at an advantage over others not using this medium for their résumés?

22. Design an online résumé for a job you are interested in. Post your résumé to online services.

23. Use one of the online job centers (pgs. 160-162) from Chapter 9 to find several jobs you would be interested in. Research the companies the jobs are with.

24. You are preparing for an interview with a company. Your preparation includes learning as much as possible about the company. Research companies using search engines such as Excite. Visit their Home Page and write a short description of the company that presents important information that you should know for your interview.

Using the Internet as an Information Resource
For the following actvities, refer to Chapter 5—Using the Internet for Business Research (pages 71-86).

25. Research information on the new role for managers—the manager as a coach. Include Usenet newsgroups as an information source. Write a short report on your findings and reference your Internet resources.

26. The company you work for has decided to use their computer network for training. You have been asked to develop a workshop on using the Internet for training. Visit training and development Web sites (pgs. 135-136) to begin your research on this topic.

27. The Internet has stimulated new discussions on copyright. Information is freely available to be downloaded, copied, and re-purposed. Artists, musicians, writers, educators, businesses, and software developers are among the many who express concerns about having their work illegally copied. Discussions on Internet copyright

are prolific. Some Internet users believe, "If you don't want your product copied, then don't put it on the Internet." Still others hold to "fair-use" standards — if the information is being used for educational purposes and not for your profit, this falls into the fair-use category and is acceptable.

In business you will use the Internet to access information. How you use that information will vary. Before you begin using Internet information for business purposes, you first need to understand copyright issues and how they are being applied to the Internet. Use the search tools you have learned about and research copyright issues on the Internet. Begin your research by visiting the Copyright Web site: **http://www.benedict.com**

Management—Planning

Strategic Management

The Internet is the fastest growing communications medium that we have ever experienced. Individuals and businesses—from Fortune 500 companies to small sole proprietorships—are establishing a presence on the Internet in the belief that cyberspace holds the potential for new profits, new customers, and a new way to conduct business.

1. The company that you work for is interested in learning more about whether they should establish an Internet presence. They present you with the following statements
    - Business on the Net is not easy.
    - Many dollars are wasted on Internet advertising.
    - The Internet is a place you can't afford not to be right now. It's not so much that you're going to [profit] in the short term; rather, you'll lose money in the long term by not being there.
    - If you're not an active Internet citizen by the mid-1990's, you're likely to be out of business by the year 2000.
    - A Web site can provide you with a global presence with one click of the mouse.
    - Putting up a Web site is like setting up shop in the middle of the desert.

Your assignment—research business practices on the Internet. Begin by exploring businesses on Net (pgs. 118-120). Write a report for your boss with facts and recommendations regarding your company's establishing an Internet presence. How does this project fit with strategic planning for the company?

2. Your company decides to proceed with the development of a World Wide Web site. How might the process of strategy formulation and implementation be used for this work?

Planning Tools and Techniques
3. *Environmental scanning.* Techniques for scanning the environment include reading newspapers, magazines, books, competitor's ads and promotional materials, attending trade shows, and debriefing sales personnel. In this activity you will use a new technique—surfing the Internet—to scan the environment for information on how to profit from providing information services on the Internet.

Few people are willing to pay for information, services, and resources on the Internet because so much of the Internet has been free. Mosaic, the first Internet browser, was given away free to those that visited its Web site. Netscape Navigator followed suit with free versions available online. Other browsers continue to be available at no charge if downloaded online. Many software application programs offer a free copy for a trial period. Many newspapers, periodicals, and journals have free online versions. News and sports can be found free at many online Web sites such as CNN, Time Warner's Pathfinder, ESPN, and *The New York Times*.

The future is changing however, as many of these sites now offer a free version of their information services, but also offer a subscription service. To begin to understand how the Internet can be used for business and perhaps most importantly for profit, it is important to learn what types of services Net users are willing to pay for. Begin learning about the future of business online by visiting the top five commercial information providers.

- Dow Jones News/Retrieval
  http://bis.dowjones.com or Telnet to **djnr.dowjones.com**

- Knight-Ridder Information/Dialog
  http://www.dialog.com or Telnet to **dialog.com**

- Knight-Ridder Information/DataStar
  http://www.www.rs.ch or Telnet to **rserve.rs.ch**

- LEXIS-NEXIS
  http://www.lexisnexis.com or Telnet to **lex.meaddata.com**

- NewsNet
  http://www.newsnet.com or Telnet to **newsnet.com**

After you have visited these sites, write a pager on "Riding the Internet Wave to Profits." Include information on

- What service is provided?
- Why will people pay for this service?
- What is the advantage of using this service for information over using traditional media?
- What capabilities does the Internet have to attract customers?

4. Benchmarking. Companies may spend thousands of dollars on putting up and maintaining a World Wide Web site. These same companies frequently find that there is little or no return for the money spent. How can benchmarking be used to help a company begin to make a profit from their Web site?

Management—Organizing
Managing Work Force Diversity
Begin your study of diversity by visiting this award winning Web site
http://www.efn.org/~dennis_w/race.html

1. Discuss the role of the Internet in providing information on diversity, and ethnocentrism.

2. Do you view these ethnocentric sites as important sources of information for managers? Why?

3. You have accepted a position at a company as a diversity manager. How will you use the Internet to prepare for your new job?

4. How can managers create a culture that advocates and encourages diversity?

5. Visit the following Web site: **http://www.afroam.org**
   Explore issues and information of importance to the African-American community. Would the type of information available at this site be of benefit to a manager? Why? Why not?

6. CASE STUDY: You have just been hired to develop a diversity training program for a company. You have been asked to develop units on African-Americans, Asian-Americans, Hispanics, and Native Americans. You decide that the first step in learning more about these cultures is to conduct research on each of these cultures. Visit the World Wide Web sites listed below to begin your research.

Afro Americ@	**http://www.afroam.org**
Hispanics	**http://www.clark.net/pub/jgbustam/ heritage/herative.html**

   http://web.maxwell.syr.edu/nativeweb/geography/latinam/ mexico/mex_main.html

Native Web	**http://web.maxwell.syr.edu/nativeweb**

7. Visit the other cultural diversity resources listed in Chapter 7. Use Internet search engines to further your knowledge.

8. When you have finished conducting your research, write a paper on cultural information that might tend to influence communication with African-Americans, Hispanics, Native Americans, and Asian-Americans. This information might include differences in attitudes, behaviors, and communication styles

9. How do communication styles differ with each of these cultures?

10. Based on your research of African-Americans, Asian-Americans, Hispanics, and Native Americans design and write a training activity whose objective is the appreciation of cultural differences as assets for making the company stronger, more creative, and more productive.

Management—Leading

Teams

1. Visit the IBM site (**http://www.hursley.ibm.com/facer/fac-docs.html**) and learn about teams at IBM. What is the purpose or goal of the IBM team? How does IBM's concept of teams support new management paradigms for the changing organization? What is the role of the "new manager"? Compare the "new management" style with the old "in charge" style.

2. Visit links to other companies from the IBM site. Discuss how teams are changing the role of managers at these companies.

3. How do teams contribute to global competitive leadership?

4. What skills do managers need to possess to succeed in a team environment?

5. How do you view Motorola's empowerment initiative affecting management?

Leadership

6. Subscribe to the listserv mailing list LDRSHP to learn more about the application of leadership theory to practice in the real world. This

unmoderated list discusses topics such as transformational leadership, development of leadership, the practice of leadership, and research of leadership.

To subscribe send an e-mail message to:
LISTSERV@iubvm.ucs.indiana.edu

In the body of your message type: **SUB LDRSHP** <your name>
If you have not subscribed to a listserv or newsgroup before, be sure to read Tips for New Users of Newsgroups and Listservs (pgs. 214-215).

Maintain your subscription to the listserv for at least two weeks. Write a short paper on what you have learned about leadership from the list. How does it differ from what you learned in your book and in class? Do you feel a listserv can be a valuable resource for you? Why or why not?

7. Bill Gates of Microsoft and Herb Kelleher of Southwest Airlines (**http://www.iflyswa.com**) are considered to be transformational leaders. Research their names and/or companies using your research skills. What information can be found on the Internet about these individuals? What can you learn about their leadership at their companies' Web sites? You may need to compare their companies' Web sites with other companies before you can make any assumptions about how their leadership styles may or may not have affected their Web sites.

8   Learn about Dr. Gilbert Amelio's leadership initiatives at Apple Computer (**http://www.apple.com**). What does this tell you about Dr. Amelio's leadership style?

9. Visit the Web site "Harrison on Leadership" at **http://www.altika.com/leadership**. Explore his collections of thoughts on leadership. Write a short paper on your thoughts about one of the following topics

- Leadership in the year 2000
- How technology can facilitate leadership
- Thoughts on success
- Spirit in business
- Innovation and creativity through leadership

10. You have been asked to develop an inservice training program on leadership. Visit the leadership Web sites and explore them for the latest information on this topic.

11. Visit the Edith Cowan University's Women and Leadership Web site. Write a short paper on women's leadership styles or women in leadership roles.

Communication and Interpersonal Skills

1. Work in small groups. Discuss whether e-mail is appropriate for each of the following good-news and goodwill information messages: order acknowledgments, letters of credit, adjustment letters, positive personal letters, thank-you messages, congratulatory letters, condolence letters, greetings and informative letters. What are the advantages/disadvantages of using electronic media for good-news and goodwill messages?

2. Divide your group in half. Select one type of good-news or goodwill information message. Group 1 will write the message to be delivered by e-mail; Group 2 writes the message to be delivered by surface mail. Compare and contrast the differences in both types of messages.

3. Many good-news and informative letters are responses to inquiries. Goodwill can be communicated by the speed at which a company responds to an inquiry request. Visit Internet business sites and evaluate how this new medium is changing or has the potential to change the quality of goodwill and customer service for information requests.

4. Work in small groups. As more individuals and companies become connected to the Internet, e-mail is rapidly becoming the preferred

way communicate. Begin by discussing the ramifications of using e-mail vs. surface mail for the following bad news and negative messages involving: orders, credit, claims, requests, invitations, and personnel issues. Will the message(s) be perceived differently when delivered by e-mail vs. surface mail? When would e-mail be appropriate? Inappropriate? Would your choice of e-mail to communicate bad news be different when writing to a manager, co-worker, or subordinate?

5. Read and discuss the following e-mail message. Why do you think that it is easy for e-mail to have a negative or angry tone? How could this situation be handled differently? Is e-mail the best way to communicate in a situation such as this? Re-write this e-mail message.

> *I thought I left you a detailed voice mail message regarding the diversity training program. I was surprised that you did not respond due to the urgency of the situation. First of all only 4 managers showed up for the meeting, not 9 as you stated in your report. Yes I too was upset by the lack of interest shown by the managers but they should be motivated to attend these types of meetings. Please return my call and report to me your thoughts and opinions on why so few showed up.*

6. Companies that are internally networked frequently use e-mail to deliver messages to employees. Ask several individuals in your group to write a bad news message to be delivered by e-mail for one of the following situations

- employees will not receive a raise this year
- a job applicant is not qualified for a management position
- an employee is denied promotion
- a company no longer can provide financial support for a holiday party
- an employee's vacation request is denied
- a warrantee replacement part for a computer is backordered for one month

Have the group respond to this message. How would they feel? Could the message have been written better for e-mail delivery? Would the tone of the message be different for a business letter?

Management—Controlling

1. Learn more about reengineering by visiting the following Web sites:
    http://www.lia.co.za/users/johannh/index.htm
    http://Is0020.fee.uva.nl/bpr

    Compare TQM with reengineering for managing change within an organization. Can you find positive changes reported from companies on the Net?

2. Why has total quality management (TQM) not been successful in many companies? Learn more about TQM by visiting management Web sites with links to TQM resources. Use search tools to research TQM. Investigate listservs or newsgroups on TQM to learn more by participating in interactive discussions.

Entrepreneurship and Small Business Management

Entrepreneurs and Cyberpreneurs

Computer-based technologies have made many creative and innovative people very wealthy. We read of the Silicon Valley nerds and the Microsoft Softies who have become millionaires in a very few years. They are driven by a creative spirit to go beyond the known limits of technology—to design, develop, and produce new media and technology tools for the future. Money does not drive these new entrepreneurs, but rather the opportunity to be creative and innovative. Their lifestyles are characterized by long working hours, little or no personal life, and an almost compulsive addiction and love for the work they are doing.

This new breed of entrepreneur seldom runs and manages his own company, but rather works for either a small company or a large corporation such as Microsoft. These new entrepreneurs are rewarded for their contributions to a company.

One of the most recent examples of this new breed of young entrepreneur is Marc Andreessen, who, as an undergraduate student at the University of Illinois, created the prototype for first World Wide Web browser— Mosaic. Andreesen, James Clark, one of the founders of Silicon Graphics, Inc., and five of the original Mosaic developers formed a company in the spring of 1994. This company became Netscape Communications Corporation released the most widely used Web browser, Netscape Navigator in October 1994.

In the fall of 1995 Netscape went public, making Clark and Andreesen, millionaires overnight. Netscape continues to define and push new boundaries as they move forward now in a head-on battle with the corporate giant Microsoft to see who can dominate the hottest new medium—the Internet. Microsoft has declared war. Who will win? Microsoft—a company that controls the computer desktop, has a huge base of software, and a great deal of money for research. Or, Netscape— a young company that many believe has won the battle of the Web from the momentum it has gained from Netscape Navigator.

New media open many new doors for the young and those with an entrepreneurial spirit. In the following learning activities, you will learn more about cyberpreneurs.

For the learning adventures in this section, you will find it helpful to begin by using the following Web sites.

http://techweb.cmp.com:2090/techweb/ia/13issue/13topsites.html
http://www.owi.com/netvalue/v1i1l1.html
http://www.colorado.edu/infs/jcb/mbac6080/business.html
http://www.hbs.harvard.edu/applegate/hot_business
http://pathfinder.com/@@7PcvogYAweyjsu6N/fortune/index.html
http://www.sirius.com/~bam/jul.html
http://www.directory.net

1. Explore Web sites for businesses and corporations that are online. Compare the Web sites of large corporations with small entrepreneurial ventures.

2. Find 2-5 online entrepreneurial ventures that intrigue you. What makes their sites exceptional?

3. Make your own Top 10 list of the best uses of the Internet for business.

4. How does an entrepreneurial venture differ on the Internet from one off line?

5. Despite all the hype that the Internet is about to become the hottest commercial property, there is one warning for those who think they may want to become cyberpreneurs—*business on the Net is not easy*. In fact, many dollars are wasted on Internet advertising. Much of the advertising done on the Internet is of poor quality and attracts very little profitable business. It's safe to say that new business ventures on the Internet will probably not make a lot of money during their first six months.

   Why should anyone consider establishing a business presence on the Internet?

6. Why do you think that few companies are making money on the Internet? What challenge does this present to the cyberpreneur?

7. How a company pays for advertising on the Internet is still being experimented with and defined. Typically, an advertiser rents a space on a Web site for a flat rate. However, some of the hottest Web sites are now experimenting with a click-through-rate. What this means is that the owner of the Web site receives money from the advertiser only if Net surfers click on the ad. Each click translates into dollars. Many believe that Net surfers ignore online adds and in fact find them annoying. They believe that few are interested in these innocuous bill-boards, quickly clicking their way to something more

interesting than an online ad. What do you think the future holds for online advertising?

8. How can a company entice Net surfers to learn more about their product from their online billboard?

9. Visit business Web sites for companies that have done creative online advertising (see pgs. 118-120 for links to online companies). Begin with Zima Clearmalt. **http://www.zima.com/zimag.html**

   Another site to visit to explore some of the best multinational companies is **http://web.idirect.com/~tiger/worldbea.htm**

   Identify 5 companies who have online advertising that is unique and that you feel may attract Net surfers. Why are these sites unique? What ideas do you have about online advertising and marketing after visiting these sites?

10. Use the Internet to research 2-3 successful entrepreneurs, such as Bill Gates, Steve Jobs, and Marc Andreesen, who are involved with computer-based technologies and new media. Summarize what characteristics these men and woman possess that enabled them to be successful.

11. What are some new opportunities that the Internet makes available to entrepreneurs?

Ethics and Social Responsibility

1. Use Ben & Jerry's Web site as a starting point to discuss how you feel about cause-related marketing. Is this just another profit-maximizing behavior? Visit other Web sites such as Reebok (**http://planetreebok.com**) and Ford (**http://www.ford.com**) to see how they differ in their corporate approach to cause-related marketing.

2. What are your beliefs about the social responsibility of a cyberpreneur?

3. How do you feel about honesty in advertising?

4. Much has been written and discussed about free speech on the Internet. In the June of 1996 three judges called Government attempts to regulate content on the Internet a "profoundly repugnant" affront to the First Amendment's guarantee of free speech and granted a temporary restraining order that prohibits the Justice Department from enforcing violations of the Communications Decency Art's ban on indecent and offensive speech. How do you feel about free speech on the Internet? How do free speech issues relate to Internet business?

5. Have an inclass debate on issues related to employee privacy. One topic to start with is the pros and cons of managers reading and having access to employees' e-mail.

6. The world's largest computer network, once the haven of scientists, hackers, and nerds, is now being overrun with millions of new users, many of whom see dollar signs when they consider entering the new frontiers of cyberspace. Many believe that the Internet is being invaded by forces that threaten to destroy the very qualities that have fueled its growth.

    Early in 1994 two lawyers from Phoenix, Arizona, Laurence Canter and Martha Siegel, did the unspeakable—they advertised on the Internet. Their simple and straightforward advertisement offered their services to aliens interested in getting a green card. All over the world, Internet uses responded with angry electronic mail messages called "flames". This husband and wife team soon became the most hated couple in cyberspace as this act stirred up international controversy that continues to be debated today.

    Since then Canter and Siegel have declared their venture "a tremendous success" claiming to have generated over $100,000 in new business in addition to royalties from their book.

    Are Canter and Siegel entrepreneurs? Explain. Have an inclass discussion or debate on this topic.

7. How do you feel about the advertising on the Internet?

8. Internet ethics—the rules that govern behavior on the Net—were set by professors, computer hackers, and brilliant hippies from the Woodstock and Vietnam era. These professors and students were from UCLA, UC Santa Barbara, Stanford, and the University of Utah. Later, hackers from Berkeley, M.I.T., and other colleges breathed life into the Internet. These early creators of the Internet largely eschewed formal rules. Their tenet was "all information should be free."

   Today's managers deal with the issue of how much information and when to provide information. How does the Internet create new information problems for managers? Begin by discussing the problems associated with the Internet grapevine within an organization.

9. A rumor is circulating on e-mail that one of the clerical staff is having an affair with the general manager. What should management do about this? How far can management go to discover the origin of the message or who is circulating it?

10. As you begin to use the Internet for research, you will find that many of the search results returned to you from search engines are companies advertising their products. For example, if you entered the words "business management" you would get a listing of many companies that have business management services. It is becoming more difficult to find useful and relevant information with search engines when there are also companies that provide services in these areas. Are businesses cluttering access to information? How do you think this will impact access to useful information on the Internet in the future? Do companies have an ethical and/or social responsibility to also provide useful information for Net surfers?

11. Select one business Web site that you have found that you believe is a good model for setting up shop on the Internet.

12. You are starting a small business and need to write a policy statement on the following: substance abuse, sexual harassment, and aids. Use the Internet as a resource for researching information that will help you write these policy statements. Write one policy statement for each of these issues.

13. Create a credo for a fictitious company you would like to start. Is it important for potential customers to know your credo? Why? If so, how would you make Net visitors to your Web site aware of your credo?

Creativity

1. Some of the most appealing Internet sites that invite Net visitors to explore their virtual environments have been developed by creative minds who understand the power and capabilities of the Internet as a new medium for communication and for information dissemination and access. Visit the Cool Web sites on pages 113-118 to explore creative uses of these technologies. Write a paper titled "Internet Creativity and Entrepreneurship."

2. *Wired* magazine (**http://www.hotwired.com**)has broken all the rules for publishing and producing print materials with their well done and popular publication. Visit their online site to see how this creative team continues to explore and push the medium to new limits. How does *Wired* illustrate the entrepreneurial spirit? How do you feel about this site as a creative entrepreneurial venture? Why do you believe that *Wired* has been so successful?

3. The new Internet business paradigm is about SERVICE over PRODUCT. How can the creative process be applied to generate a Web site for a company that will attract potential Web customers?

4. Entrepreneurs must always be on guard against outdated paradigms. One old paradigm that is a challenge for businesses is related to marketing strategies. Discuss the new advertising paradigm for the Internet—SERVICE before PRODUCT. What are the challenges for Internet advertising? What are the opportunities?

5. Questions are extremely valuable in the quest for creativity. Work in small groups and formulate 10 thought-provoking questions that your team will address before designing a Web site for a new small business.

6. In your group planning for the development of a Web site, think of 10 names for the Web site that will attract Net surfers. Take notes as to why you think each name would be appropriate.

7. How can you use the Internet to stimulate creativity?

8. In an interview with *Wired* magazine in August 1996, Peter Drucker was quoted as saying, "The most successful innovators are the creative imitators" What does he mean by this?

Transforming Ideas Into Reality

In the next activities you will be transforming your ideas for a Web site for a small business into a blueprint design. You may want to visit several Web sites and learn more about cyberpreneurs before you begin. Start with these sites

http://www.cyberpreneur.com
http://sulcus.berkeley.edu/Invention
http://emporium.turnpike.net:80/B/bizopp/index.html
http://asa.ugl.lib.umich.edu/chdocs/cyberpreneur/Cyber.html

1. Now that you have visited and explored businesses on the Web and learned about creative design for communication and information access, you are ready to think of ideas for an entrepreneurial venture on the Internet. Work in small groups and brainstorm ideas. Identify the good ideas and select one.

2. What criteria must be met before your idea can become a viable business opportunity? What criteria must be met before an Internet business venture can hope to be successful? What are potential sources for opportunity on the Internet not available elsewhere?

3. Conduct a screening of your idea to analyze its potential. What questions must be asked to evaluate this opportunity? What questions must be asked to evaluate success factors?

4. Identify the sources of risk in this venture. How can these potential risks be reduced?

5. Can you identify businesses on the Internet that you believe may have trouble being successful? Why? If these sites have e-mail addresses, write to them and ask them about the success of their Web ventures.

6. Identify businesses on the Internet that you believe may be successful. What have they done on their Web site to attract customers and potential business?

7. Identify other ideas for Internet businesses by visiting these Web sites:
   http://www.IdeaCafe.com
   http://www.catalog.com/impulse/invent
   http://www20.mindlink.net/interweb/bestbusinesses.html

8. Are you an idea killer? Take the Personal Killer Phrase quiz at this unique site **http://redlt.com/idea**

Marketing Assessment and Strategies

1. Successful entrepreneurs are skilled at conducting market assessments. How will you assess your Internet market? How will this assessment differ from a traditional market assessment?

2. Use demographic data available on the Internet to help assess your market. Visit these demographic sites to learn more about Internet demographics.
   http://etrg.findsvp.com/features/newinet.html
   http://WWW.Stars.com/Vlib/Misc/Statistics.html
   http://www-personal.umich.edu/~sgupta/hermes/survey3
   http://www.cc.gatech.edu/gvu/user_surveys

Review and analyze the data and write a short report on the conclusions you have reached based on the Internet demographics as it applies to your business idea. Can you assess the market for your product based on these survey results?

3. What major forces, trends, or events could alter the technological future of your Web venture over the next 2-5 years?

4. Visit two of the following World Wide Web sites. Observe how they are communicating with their customers and Web visitors. How is the Internet being used as a tool for businesses to communicate with customers?

    AT&T **http://www.att.com/net**
    Fidelity Investment **http://www.fid-inv.com**
    Southwest Airlines **http://www.iflyswa.com**
    Time Warner's Pathfinder **http://pathfinder.com**

    Write a short paper where you discuss the use of the Internet as a new technology for business communication.

5. How are you going to use the Internet to provide customer service?

The Marketing Plan

1. Many companies can help you create a business presence on the Internet. Their services include creating a Web Home Page, and Web ads, and recommending an appropriate location for the Web page. To see an example of an Internet marketing service connect to the Downtown Anywhere site. **http://awa.com**

    What services do they provide? What are the advantages? Disadvantages? Would you consider using such a service?

2. Visit this Web site for information on businesses hosting Web directories **http://www.directory.net**

    Would this Web resource be useful for you?

3. Other sources for making your Web site known to others is having your site listed with search directories and search engines. Visit the Home Pages for 5 search tools and investigate how to submit your Web page.

4. How are you going to effectively market your Internet venture?

5. How will you generate income from your venture?

6. How will you use the Internet to advertise your product/service?

7. How has the Internet changed the way business is conducted? Provide examples.

8. What is your favorite business Web site? Why? What have you learned from exploring businesses on the Internet? What surprised you the most? What disappointed you the most?

9. Explore entrepreneur and small business Web sites on pages 137-146 to learn about the resources available to you to continue learning about cyberpreneurship and small Internet business ventures.

10. What was your favorite small business or entrepreneur Web site? Why?

Global Business

1. Visit this Web site (**http://ciber.bus.msu.edu/busres/company.htm**) and find 10 of the world's largest industrial and service companies. Use this site to research the companies. Select one of the companies that interests you the most to write about. Write about the company from the perspective of international management.

    Another site to visit to find online multinational companies (MNC) is **http://web.idirect.com/~tiger/worldbea.htm**

2. Select one MNC. Use Internet resources to research the country where this company is located. Learn about the culture and environment for this company. How do you think the cultural setting and environment affects the management practices?

3. Visit this Web site **http://ciber.bus.msu.edu/busres/company.htm** and select the link to Fortune 500. Explore and learn about world's largest industrial and service companies. From your Internet research of the world's largest MNCs, write a paper on "How Businesses Compete in the Information Age."

   NOTE...The information at this site is offered in "PDF" (Portable Document Format). You can view them by using Adobe's reader (available free by clicking on the link to Adobe's FTP site). After downloading the reader, install it as a helper application in your browser's preferences. Then, simply select and PDF file to download and read.

4. Download and print the Global 500 Excel spreadsheet to learn more about these MNCs. What can you learn from this data about the world's largest industrial and service companies? Discuss in small groups.

5. Visit International Business Resources on the Web page
   http://ciber.bus.msu.edu/busres/company.htm
   Make a list of the 10 Best International Business Web Sites. Present the information to the class and discuss the benefits of each site for international business.

6. If you were a small company interested in international trade, what information would you find valuable at the Europages site?
   http://www.europages.com/g/home.html

7. Chief Executive Officer of Oracle Corp, Raymond Land, has transformed Oracle into a stable and profitable global corporation with a franchise approaching that of giant Microsoft Corporation.

Use Internet resources to research and learn more about Oracle. Be sure to use the exceptional Internet resource from the Wall Street Journal. **http://www.wsrn.com**

8. Visit the Web site for International Chamber of Commerce (ICC) **http://www1.usa1.com/~ibnet/icchp.html**

   How can ICC benefit international businesses? What services do they provide? How can ICC benefit environmental managers, advertising and marketing executives?

9. How can this Web site help a company interested in international exports and imports? **http://trading.wmw.com**

10. Visit this Web site and explore these excellent resources for international business. **http://ciber.bus.msu.edu/busres.htm**

    How would you use this resource to find information about a country's economy?

11. What is the hottest international trade spot? **http://rampages.onramp.net/~tradelaw/asiabusiness.html**

12. Your company has a product to sell. How do you find a trade spot? **http://rampages.onramp.net/~tradelaw/europebus.html**

13. The Internet has changed international trade and law. Learn about the future of international trade by visiting this Web site http://rampages.onramp.net/~modact/news.html

    What happens to international trade when we can transmit information cheaply and quickly to any place on earth?

14. What valuable resources does the Internet offer to the international trade community?

15. What is the potential for international trade on the Internet?

16. How can software be protected from illegal copying and distribution in countries like China and Russia? Research patents, trademarks, and copyright. Begin by visiting this award-winning copyright site **http://www.benedict.com**

    The URL for the patents site is: **http://sunsite.unc.edu/patents/intropat.html**

17. How are MNCs promoting themselves globally via the World Wide Web **http://web.idirect.com/~tiger/worldbea.htm**

18. Visit the Home Pages of globally active companies. What can you learn about Home Page design to help make a business Web site better?

19. What is your favorite Web site for a large multinational manufacturing company? Why? What attracts potential customers to their site?

20. What is your favorite multinational service company Web site? Why? What attracts potential customers to their site?

21. What is your favorite small or medium size multinational Web site? Why? What attracts potential customers to their site?

22. Many companies are spending thousands of dollars creating a Web presence. Are they getting their money's worth? Are the Web sites for the large multinational companies more effective for attracting potential customers than the sites for the small or medium MNCs?

23. For a different perspective on finding multinational companies, visit **http://www.wincorp.com:80/windata/index.html**

    Compare the two sites and how they provide information services to the business community.

24. Visit the business Netiquette site and learn about etiquette for international business communication. Write 10 guidelines for communicating with international companies by electronic mail.

25. How does international communication differ from communication in America?

26. How can the Internet be used to improve communication between people of different cultures?

27. How can the Internet be used to learn more about cultural differences when managing an international business? List 5 of the best Web sites for learning about culture, cultural diversity, and the cultural setting.

28. Research the culture of a country you would be interested in working in. How does this culture differ from our culture? Will this cultural complexity affect the management of a business in this country?

29. Providing direction and purpose for a culturally diverse work force in an MNC is a challenging task. What can you learn about management in an MNC such as IBM
http://www.hursley.ibm.com/facer/fac-docs.html

30. Make a Top 10 List for the best Internet resources for international business. Write a brief descriptor with information on the value of each site.

31. Use the following Web sites to explore multinational companies. What can you learn about their company philosophy, corporate culture, or values? List 5 companies.

    http://ciber.bus.msu.edu/busres/company.htm
    http://www.wincorp.com:80/windata/index.html
    http://web.idirect.com/~tiger/worldbea.htm

CHAPTER 9
Using Cyberspace for Career Planning

Today more and more career development centers are using the Internet as a resource for career planning. Major career planning activities include self-assessment and career exploration. In this chapter, you will

- ➡ take a self-awareness journey to learn more about yourself and your personal and professional needs.
- ➡ research jobs that fit you as a person.
- ➡ learn how to use the Internet for career exploration: communication with people, electronic publications, career resources, and professional services.

Self-Awareness Journey

Self-assessment is the first step in career planning. Self-assessment is an important process that requires inner reflection. The goal of this reflective process is to help you develop a better understanding of your interests, talents, values, goals, aptitudes, abilities, personal traits, and desired lifestyle. You will use this information to help you find a job that fits you as a person. This personal survey is very important in helping you become aware of the interrelationship between your personal needs and your occupational choices.

Start by identifying:

- your interests and what is important to you;
- what you enjoy doing in your free time;
- skills you learned in the classroom or from an internship that are related to your career interests;

- your accomplishments;
- abilities and capabilities;
- work experience related to your career interests;
- personal traits and characteristics;
- your strengths and weaknesses; and
- physical and psychological needs.

Ask these questions regarding career considerations:

- Where would you like to live? In a city, the suburbs, the country, the seashore, or the mountains?

- Is there a specific geographic location where you would like to live?

- How do you feel about commuting to work? Would you drive a long distance to work for the advantage of living outside of a city?

- Is the community that you live in important? For example, do you value a community that is outdoor oriented or family oriented?

- What type of work environment is important to you? Do you want to wear a power suit every day or be casual?

- Is making a lot of money important to you?

- How do you feel about benefits and promotion options?

- Are flexible hours and free weekends important? For example, do you value free time to exercise and participate in outdoor activities? Are you willing to sacrifice this part of your life for a job? Would you be satisfied with making enough money to live on and have more free time?

- Do you mind working long hours each day or weekends? How do you feel about taking vacation time?

- Do you want to work for a large or small company? Would you rather work for a small company where everyone knows each other and the atmosphere is perhaps a little more casual? Or is it more important to be with a large company with many career advancement opportunities?

- Where would you like to be in your professional life in 5 years? 10 years? Does this company offer advancement opportunities that fit your goals?

- How do you feel about work-related travel? Do you mind traveling if a job requires you to do so? Do you mind giving up portions of your weekend to travel? How many days a month are you willing to be away from home?

- How do you feel about being a member of a work team?

After you have completed your self-awareness journey, you are ready to use this information to explore career options.

Career Exploration

The goal of career exploration is to help you to find job opportunities that match your personal and professional needs. Career exploration involves gathering information about the world of work. You will eliminate or select jobs based on what you learned in your self-assessment. For example, if you determine that location is an important factor when selecting a job, you would use this criterion to select or eliminate job opportunities based on where a particular company is located. Information about the work environment and corporate culture will be more difficult to obtain.

There are many ways to obtain information about the world of work. In this section we will explore several options involving communication and the use of the Internet to acquire information.

People as Information Resources

Internships and work experience provide excellent opportunities to learn about companies and their world of work. For example, if you are doing an internship for a company, observe the work ethic and corporate environment. Ask someone doing a job that interests you what it is like to work for the company. How many hours do they work per day? Are they expected to work weekends? How do their department, boss, and other employees view vacations? Do they have free time during a day for personal interests such as running, cycling, or working out at the gym? What are the company's expectations of its employees? If a job position requires the employee to travel, ask how many days per month they travel. When do they leave to travel; when do they return? How are they compensated for overtime?

Other sources for obtaining information from people include

- talking with your career counselors;
- attending seminars and workshops where you can interact with professionals and ask questions;
- attending conventions and job fairs;
- joining a professional organization; and
- NETWORK, NETWORK, NETWORK!

Publications as Information Resources

Professional publications provide valuable information about the world of work. Check with your career counselor or professors for publications that will provide useful information. Visit **Madalyn**—the Web site from the University of Deleware MBA Program—to find many links to current business news. **http://www.udel.edu/alex/mba/main/netdir2.html**

The **Electronic Newsstand** is another excellent resource with many links to electronic versions of publications. **http://www.enews.com**

The Internet as an Information Resource

The Internet has many valuable resources for learning about the world of work. Resources include:

- World Wide Web sites of companies
- Usenet newsgroups
- listserv mailing lists
- job and career resources

World Wide Web

Many companies have World Wide Web sites. You will find many of these Web sites useful in learning about a company's products and services and, in some instances, about their work environment. Use search engines described in Chapter 5 to enter in the name of companies you are interested in to find their Home Pages. Listed below are Web sites to visit that have links to companies on the Internet.

Commercial Sites Index (http://www.directory.net) lists businesses that have set up Home Pages on the Web.

Interesting Business Sites on the Web (http://www.owi.com/netvalue/index.html) is a relatively small list of sites (less than 50) that covers most of the exciting business uses of the Web.

The LIST (http://www.sirius.com/~bam/jul.html) is an excellent Web site with links to online businesses.

Usenet Newsgroups

In the virtual community of the Internet, Usenet newsgroups are analogous to cybercafés where people with similar interests gather from around the world to interact and exchange ideas. Usenet is a very large distributed bulletin board system (BBS) that has several thousand specialized discussion groups. Currently there are over 20,000 newsgroups with about 20 to 30 more added weekly. Anyone can start a newsgroup.

> **NOTE**
>
> Your college or university must carry Usenet News before you can use your Internet browser to read and interact with newsgroups.

Listed below are several Usenet newsgroups that are relevant to job searching and career planning:

misc.jobs.contract
misc.jobs.misc
misc.jobs.offered
misc.jobs.offered.entry
misc.jobs.resumes

Netscape Navigator supports Usenet newsgroups. To view all the newsgroups available on your college or university network, follow these steps from within Netscape Navigator 2.0:

1. Click on the **Window** pull-down menu.
2. Select **Netscape News**.
3. Within the Netscape News window, go to the **Options** pull-down menu.
4. Select **Show All Newsgroups**.

Visit this Web site for a listing of Usenet newsgroups:
http://ibd.ar.com/ger

Visit this Web site and use a simple search tool to locate Usenet newsgroups of interest. **http://www.cen.uiuc.edu/cgi-bin/find-news**

For more information on using Netscape for reading newsgroups, refer to *Netscape Adventures—Step-by-Step Guide to Netscape Navigator and the World Wide Web*.

Listserv Mailing Lists

A *listserv* is the automated mailing system that distributes electronic mail. Mailing lists provide a forum where individuals of shared interests can exchange ideas and information; any members of the group may participate in the resulting discussion. This is no longer a one-to-one communication like your e-mail, but rather a one-to-many communication. Electronic mail written in the form of a report, article, abstract, reaction, or comment is received at a central site and is then distributed to the members of the list.

Finding a Listserv for Jobs and Career Planning
There are several Internet resources to help you to find a listserv mailing list for jobs or career planning.
http://www.yahoo.com/Business_and_Economy/Employment/ Mailing_Lists

Two World Wide Web sites for finding mailing lists are:
http://www.liszt.com
http://www.tile.net/tile/listserv/index.html

Travel to this excellent Gopher server and follow the path to information on current mailing lists. You can also do a search for mailing lists by subject.

Gopher:	**liberty.uc.wlu.edu**
path:	Explore Internet Resources/Searching for Listservs

You can also use electronic mail to request information on listserv mailing lists on a particular topic. Send an e-mail message to:

LISTSERV@vm1.nodak.edu

In the message body, type: **LIST GLOBAL /keyword**

For example, if you were looking for a mailing list on jobs you would type in the message body: **LIST GLOBAL/jobs**

TIPS for New Users of Newsgroups and Listservs

Tip 1...

After you subscribe to a list or newsgroup, don't send anything to it until you have been reading the messages for at least one week. This will give you an opportunity to observe the tone of the list and the types of messages that people are sending. Newcomers to lists often ask questions that were discussed at length several days or weeks before.

Tip 2...

Remember that everything you send to the list or newsgroup goes to every subscriber on the list. Many of these discussion groups have thousands of members. Before you reply or post a message, read and review what you have written. Is your message readable and free of errors and typos? When necessary, AMEND BEFORE YOU SEND.

Tip 3...

Look for a posting by someone who seems knowledgeable about a topic. If you want to ask a question, look for their e-mail address in the signature information at the top of the news article. Send your question to them directly rather than to the entire newsgroup or listserv.

Tip 4...

Proper etiquette for a mailing list is to not clog other people's mail boxes with information not relevant to them. If you want to respond to mail on the list or newsgroup, determine whether you want your response to go only to the individual who posted the mail or to go to all the list's subscribers. The person's name and e-mail address will be listed in their posting signature.

Tip 5...

The general rule for posting a message to a list or newsgroup is to keep it short and to the point. Most subscribers do not appreciate multiple-page postings.

If you are contacting an individual by electronic mail, identify yourself, state why you are contacting them, and indicate where you found their posting. Again, be as succinct and to the point as possible.

Request further information by either e-mail or by phone.

Job and Career Resources on the Internet

There are many excellent career planning and job-related resources on the Internet. Listed below are a few Web sites to investigate.

CareerMosaic—Follow the links to the Resource Center
http://www.careermosaic.com

Career Magazine
http://www.careermag.com/careermag

Monster Board Resource Link
http://199.94.216.76:80/jobseek/center/cclinks.htm

Occupational Outlook Handbook
http://www.jobweb.org/occhandb.htm

Online Career Center
http://www.occ.com

■ **Riley Guide**
http://www.jobtrak.com/jobguide/what-now.html

■ **Survival Guide For College Graduates**
http://lattanze.loyola.edu/MonGen/home.html

■ **Tripod**—Tools for life to help you prepare for the real world
http://www.tripod.com/tripod/

■ **US Industrial Outlook**—Information on job market realities
http://www.jobweb.org/indoutlk.htm

Professional Services as Information Resources

One valuable service to job seekers who want to learn what it's really like to work at a specific company or within a specific industry is Wet Feet Press. This service provides comprehensive in-depth analyses of companies at a cost of $25 per report. If you are currently enrolled as a Bachelor's or Master's student at a Wet Feet Press "Information Partnership" university, your cost is only $15 per report. As an alumnus of these universities, the cost is $20 per report. For more information call 1-800-926-4JOB. Visit the career center at your university or college to see if it belongs to Information Partners. For information on becoming an Information Partners member, call 415-826-1750.

The National Business Employment Weekly

The National Business Employment Weekly, published by Dow Jones & Company, Inc., is the nation's preeminent career guidance and job-search publication. It offers all regional recruitment advertising from its parent publication, *The Wall Street Journal*, as well as timely editorials on how to find a new job, manage the one you have, or start a business. You will find information on a wide range of careers. You will also get the latest on business and franchising opportunities, and special reports on workplace diversity. To view additional NBEW articles, subscription information, and job hunters' résumés, go to **http://www.occ.com/occ**

CHAPTER 10
Using Cyberspace to Find a Job

In this chapter, you will learn how to

- find companies with job opportunities.
- use the Internet as a tool for learning about job resources.
- develop résumés to showcase talent and skill.
- find Internet sites to post your résumé with.
- use the Internet as a tool to maximize your potential for finding a job.
- prepare for a job interview by researching prospective companies.

The Internet provides new opportunities for job-seekers and companies to find good employment matches. Many companies are turning to the Internet believing that the people who keep up with the most current information and technological advances in their field are the best candidates for positions. The growing perception among employers is that they may be able to find better candidates if they search online.

The types of jobs offered on the Internet have changed dramatically over the last ten years. In the past, job announcements were primarily academic or in the field of science and technology. Now, thousands of positions in all fields from graphic artists to business and marketing professionals, from medical professionals to Internet surfers and Web programmers, are being advertised.

Many companies realize the impact of the digital revolution on business and are searching for professionals who are already online cybersurfing, networking with peers, researching information, asking questions, and learning collaboratively from others around the world. A number of companies report difficulty finding such qualified individuals.

How Can the Internet Help Me Find a Job?

The Internet provides an abundance of job resources including searchable databases, résumé postings and advertising, career planning information, and job-search strategies. There are several databases and newsgroups that allow you to post your résumé at no cost. Many companies post job listings on their Web pages.

The Internet also encourages networking with people around the country and around the world. People that you meet on the Internet can be important resources for helping you to find a job and learn more about the business or career you are interested in.

Each day, the number of job openings increases as new services become available. Many believe that the real changes and opportunities are still to come. The question is no longer whether the Internet should be used to find a job or an employee, but rather, how to use it.

How Do I Begin?

Listed below are a few ways to use the Internet in your job search:

- Visit Web sites with business resources or links to online companies. For example, Intel (**http://www.intel.com**) has information on job opportunities within the company (**http://www.intel.com/intel/oppty/us.htm**) as well as information on how to submit a résumé.

- Research companies that you are interested in by finding and exploring their Web pages.

- Learn more about job resources, electronic résumés, and employment opportunities available on the Internet.

- Create an electronic résumé.

- Use the Internet to give yourself and your résumé maximum visibility.

- Participate in Usenet newsgroups and listserv mailing lists to network and learn about companies you are interested in working for.

- Learn as much as possible about a prospective company before going for a job interview.

Seven Steps to Internet Job Searching

STEP 1
Research companies or organizations that you are interested in by finding and exploring their Web pages. There are many ways to find companies to match your personal and professional needs. Use the information from your self-assessment to refine and define your search for companies. Use both online and off-line resources. Listed below are sources to assist you in finding companies.

- Go to your library and review publications in your field of study. Look for classified ads in these publications. Find names of companies that interest you. Research these companies using the search tools you learned in Chapter 5.

- Search the classified section in newspapers in the cities or regions where you would like to live. Use the Internet to research these companies.

- Use Internet search tools described in Chapter 5 to find companies and employment opportunities. Begin by using broad terms such as *employment* or *employment and business.* If you are looking for employment opportunities in business communication, you might enter in keywords that describes a job position, such as—*accountant, management training, office manager, sales*—or if you know the name of the company, do a search entering the company name as your keyword.

Visit these Web sites to find links to Internet resources for helping you to find business employment opportunities.

Infoseek Guide
http://guide.infoseek.com
Use the search engine and enter the word "employment."

World Wide Web Virtual Library
http://www.w3.org/hypertext/DataSources/bySubject/Overview.html

Yahoo
http://www.yahoo.com/yahoo/Business/Employment/Jobs/

STEP 2

Explore job resources and employment opportunities available on the Internet. Many Web sites have job postings and information on how to write résumés and effectively use the Internet for finding a job. Listed below are several excellent Internet resources to help you begin.

Best Bets for Extending Your Search: Other Internet Job Guides
http://www.lib.umich.edu/chdocs/employment/
This guide pulls together the Net's best sources of job openings and career development information, along with a description and evaluation of each resource.

Employment Opportunities and Job Resources on the Internet
http://www.jobtrak.com/jobguide
Margaret F. Riley's Web site has excellent job resources. A MUST VISIT Internet stop.

JobHunt: A Meta-list of Online Job-Search Resources and Services
http://rescomp.stanford.edu/jobs.html

☎ **Job Search and Employment Opportunities: Best Bets from the Net**, Phil Ray and Brad Taylor, University of Michigan SILS
http://asa.ugl.lib.umich.edu/chdocs/employment

☎ **Job Search Guide**
gopher://una.hh.lib.umich.edu/00/inetdirsstacks/employment %3araytay

☎ **RPI Career Resources**
http://www.rpi.edu/dept/cdc

☎ **Survival Guide for College Graduates**
http://lattanze.loyola.edu/MonGen/home.html
This award winning Web site (Fig. 8.1) has valuable information for college graduates seeking employment.

☎ **YAHOO Employment Resources**
http://www.yahoo.com/Business_and_Economy/Employment/

FIGURE 10.1
Web page for A Survival Guide for College Graduates

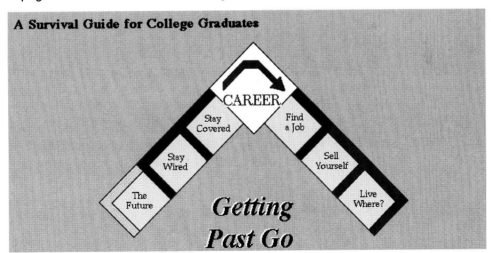

Usenet newsgroups and listserv mailing lists are two other Internet resources for learning about employment opportunities and for finding out how to find the information you are searching for.

STEP 3

Learn about electronic résumés. The World Wide Web has created opportunities for new types of résumés and business cards. Those who take advantage of the power of this new medium stand out as being technologically advanced and in touch with the future.

Listed below are Web sites to visit to examine online résumés. The individuals who have created these résumés understand how to use the medium to sell themselves. At the same time, they are stating that they have special skills for this new marketing medium that set them apart from other candidates.

Visit these Web sites and study these online résumés. Ask yourself the following questions as you look at them:

- How are online résumés different from traditional résumés?

- How do online résumés have an advantage over traditional résumés?

- What are some characteristics of the Internet as a medium that can be used to your advantage when designing a résumé to sell yourself to a company?

- How are these individuals taking advantage of the Internet as a medium to communicate?

- What do you view as advantages of using online résumés?

Sample Online Résumés and Home Pages

John Lockwood's Home Page
http://ipoint.vlsi.uiuc.edu/people/lockwood/lockwood.html

Mike Swartzbeck Home Page
http://myhouse.com/mikesite/

- Sandra L. Daine—Web designer, author, editor
  http://q.continuum.net/~shazara/resume.html

- Jon Keegan—Illustrator
  http://web.syr.edu/~jmkeegan/resume.html

- Allan Trautman—Puppeteer and actor
  http://www.smartlink.net/~trautman

- Ricardo Araiza—Student
  http://pwa.acusd.edu/~ricardo/resume.html

- Kenneth Morril—Web developer
  http://webdesk.com/resumes/kjmresume.html

- Laura Ann Wallace—Attorney
  http://lagnaf.isdn.mcs.net/~laura

Visit CareerMosaic to learn more about what online résumés look like and what they will look like in the future.
http://www.careermosaic.com/

Then go to the Career Resource Center. Send e-mail to these individuals and see if they have received job offers. Ask them about the responses they have received from their Web sites. How did they get maximum exposure to the Internet business community?

Visit Yahoo and explore links to résumé posting resources.
http://www.yahoo.com/Business_and_Economy/Employment/ Resumes

STEP 4
Visit online sites for job seekers. The next step is to visit Web sites that post résumés. Identify sites where you would like to post your résumé. There are many services available for job-seekers and for companies looking for employees. Companies usually pay to be listed; job-seekers may be allowed to post their résumés at no cost.

America's Job Bank
http://www.ajb.dni.us/index.html
This online employment service offers information on over 250,000 employment opportunities.

CareerMosaic
http://www.careermosaic.com
Begin your CareerMosaic tour by visiting the J.O.B.S. database, with thousands of up-to-date opportunities from hundreds of employers. Then stop by their USENET "jobs.offered" page to perform a full-text search of jobs listed in regional and occupational newsgroups in the U.S. and abroad. If you would also like to make your résumé accessible to interested employers from all corners of the globe, key into ResumeCM and post your résumé online.

Career Path
http://www.careerpath.com
Review employment opportunities from a number of the nation's leading daily newspapers such as *The New York Times*, *Los Angeles Times*, *The Boston Globe*, *Chicago Tribune*, *San Jose Mercury News*, and *The Washington Post*.

Career Resources Home Page
http://www.rpi.edu/dept/cdc/homepage.html
This Web site has links to online employment services including professional and university-based services.

CareerWeb
http://www.cweb.com
Search by job, location, employment, or keyword to find the perfect job. You can also browse employer profiles and search the library's list of related publications.

E-Span
http://www.espan.com
E-Span, one of the country's foremost online recruitment services, provides tools designed to meet the needs of an increasingly competitive career market. Recently added to their services is Résumé

ProKeyword Database that is available to more than 60,000 individually registered career service consumers. Visit this Web site and select Job Tools.

Helpwanted.com
http://helpwanted.com
This site offers a searchable index of job openings for companies that have paid to be listed.

IntelliMatch
http://www.intellimatch.com
Connect to IntelliMatch and fill out a résumé; hundreds of employers will have access to your profile via the Holmes search software. Review other services such as job-related sites and products, participating companies, and descriptions of available jobs.

The Internet Online Career Center
http://www.occ.com
This career center and employment database is one of the highest-volume job centers with a long list of employment opportunities and resources. Post your résumé in HTML format. Use multimedia (images, photographs, audio, and video) to enrich your résumé.

JobHunt
http://rescomp.stanford.edu/jobs/
An award-winning Web site with a meta-list of online job-search resources and services.

The Monster Board
http://www.monster.com/home.html
This unusual ad agency is a service for recruitment and furnishes information for job-seekers.

National Employment Job Bank
http://www.nlbbs.com/~najoban/
Executive Search of New England is pleased to post current career opportunities on their newest service, The National Employment Job Bank. These positions are current and represent some of the finest

employers and employment services in the country. There is never a fee charged to any applicant. These positions will be from nearly all states in the U.S.

Stanford University
http://rescomp.stanford.edu
Stanford University's site provides listings of online job services such as Medsearch and the Chronicle of Higher Education. They also have links to other agencies.

YahooJobs
http://www.yahoo.com/yahoo/Business/Employment/Jobs/
Many excellent links to help you find a job.

STEP 5
Create an online résumé to showcase your talents. In Steps 1-4, you learned about

- companies that fit your career interests;
- job and career resources on the Internet;
- electronic résumés and how they can showcase talents; and
- Web sites for job seekers.

You are now ready to use this information to create your own electronic résumé to showcase your talents and skills. Well designed, creative, and interesting online résumés set creative job seekers apart from others. When many individuals are competing for the same job, it is essential to stand apart and showcase your talents as to how they will benefit a company, especially in a time when businesses realize the importance of being networked to the world.

Creating an exceptional online résumé takes planning and careful thought. Online résumés take different forms. Some may be electronic versions of text-based résumés. Others may be home pages with links to resources that showcase a person's work and expertise.

Preparing Your Résumé for the Internet

Before you begin, think about your goals and what you would like to accomplish with an online résumé. Your primary goal is hopefully to find a job and not just to impress friends with a cool Home Page.

You will need to determine whether to create your online résumé yourself or hire a résumé service. If you are creating an electronic résumé on your own, consider whether you want to develop your own Home Page for your résumé or use an online database service to post your résumé. If you plan to create a Home Page you will need to learn HTML programming or use a software application program that creates an HTML code from your text. There are many software programs to assist you with this, as well as word processing programs that convert text to HTML.

If you are using an online résumé service, find out what type of text file they want. Usually, you will be asked for ASCII text. Most word processors and résumé writing programs have options for saving a file as ASCII or plaintext.

Investigate Résumé Services

Consider using a résumé service to create an online résumé. One advantage of using a service is that you may be able to get your résumé online quickly with instant exposure to many job opportunities. One disadvantage of using a service is that you do not have as much control over how your résumé will look. You may not be able to use complex graphics or other multimedia effects when using a service.

Cost is another limiting factor. Some companies charge a monthly fee to post your résumé, in addition to a set-up and sign-on fee. Look for companies that charge a reasonable fee to write a résumé ($35 - $50) and no fee to post it on their Web site. Investigate what other services they provide. How many visitors does this site have each day, each week? Will this site give you maximum exposure to potential employers?

Visit Web sites with résumé services and evaluate their service. How many online résumés are posted? Are the résumés well done, creative, interesting? How well do they promote the job seeker?

Whether you choose to use a résumé service or to create your own online résumé, there are seven essential elements to follow.

The Seven Essential Elements of Electronic Résumés

1. **Text must be properly formatted as an ASCII text file.**
   Using ASCII ensures that your résumé can be read universally by everyone and that readers will be able to scroll through your text. Additionally, an ASCII document can be e-mailed to anyone in the world and read.

2. **Showcase your experience and education.**
   At the top of your résumé, provide links to your experience and education. Experience is usually the first thing employers look for. A fancy résumé will not help you get a job if you do not have the right qualifications. Notice that many online résumés provide examples of their work.

3. **Provide an e-mail hyperlink.**
   An e-mail hyperlink provides an easy way for prospective employers to contact you by e-mail. By clicking on the link, they can send you a message, ask questions, or request additional information. Anything that makes it easier for recruiters improves your chances of being called for an interview.

4. **Use nouns as keywords to describe your experience.**
   When employers use the Internet to search for qualified individuals, they will frequently use search engines that require keywords. The keywords used by employers are descriptors of the essential characteristics required to do a job, such as education, experience, skills, knowledge, and abilities. The more keywords that your résumé contains, the better your chances of being found in an electronic database.

Action words such as *created, arbitrated, managed, designed,* and *administered* are out. Therefore, use words such as *manager, law enforcement, accountant, MBA.* The use of nouns will tend to produce better results.

5. **Use white space.**
An electronic résumé does not need to be one page long and single spaced. The use of white space makes reading easier and is visually more appealing. Use space to indicate that one topic has ended and another has begun.

If you are a new graduate, a résumé the equivalent of one page is appropriate. For most individuals with experience, the equivalent of two pages is the norm. Individuals who have worked in a field for many years may use two to three pages.

6. **Keep track of the number of visitors to your page.**
A counter will keep track of the number of visitors that view your page. A counter is important when paying for a résumé service, to monitor how successful the service is at getting exposure for your résumé.

7. **Be sure your page gets maximum exposure to potential employers.**
One way that employers look for prospective employees is to do a keyword search using search engines such as Yahoo, Excite, and Alta Vista. Each search engine uses different criteria for selection of Internet resources that are available in their database. Be sure that your page is listed with search engines. Visit search engine Web sites and learn how to submit your page. Additionally, investigate the selection criteria for these search engines.

Other Points to Consider

- Think of creative ways to show your talents, abilities, and skills. World Wide Web pages are excellent for linking to examples of your work.

- REMEMBER that experience is perhaps the critical element for recruiters. Be sure your résumé showcases your experience and skills in as many ways as possible.

- Visit the top 10-15 companies that you are interested in working for. Research their World Wide Web Home Page. Learn as much as possible about the company. Use this information when designing and creating your résumé to include information and skills that the company is looking for in its employees. Use this information before you go for an interview to show your knowledge and interest in the company.

- Investigate whether you will be able to submit your résumé electronically to the company.

- Are you concerned about confidentiality? Inquire about who will have access to the database you are posting your résumé with. Will you be notified if your résumé is forwarded to an employer? If the answers to these questions are not satisfactory to you, reconsider posting with this database.

- Once you post your résumé, anyone can look at it and find your address and phone number. You may want to omit your home address and just list your phone number and an e-mail hyperlink. Many recruiters and employers prefer to contact individuals by phone; if you decide not to post your phone number, you may be overlooked.

- Can your résumé be updated at no cost? You may want to add something to your résumé or correct a typo. Look for services that do not charge for updates.

- How long will your résumé be posted with the service? A good service will delete résumés after 3 to 6 months if they have not been updated.

STEP 6

Use the Internet to give yourself and your résumé maximum visibility. Successful job searches using the Internet require an aggressive approach. A résumé should be filed with many job-listing databases as well as with companies that you are interested in working for. Listed below are additional guidelines for giving yourself maximum exposure using the Internet.

- File your résumé with as many databases as possible. Visit the Net Sites for Job Seekers and find as many sites as possible to submit your résumé to.

- Use search engines and their indexes to locate resources specific to your occupation or interest.

- Visit the Home Pages of companies that you are interested in and explore their pages to find job listings. Find out if you can submit your résumé to them electronically.

- Use Usenet newsgroups and listserv mailing lists for information on finding jobs and posting your résumé.

Listed below are several Usenet newsgroups to investigate for posting résumés.

biz.jobs.offered
misc.jobs.contract
misc.jobs.misc
misc.jobs.offered
misc.jobs.offered.entry
misc.jobs.resume

STEP 7

Learn as much as possible about a prospective company before going for a job interview. Before going for a job interview, it is important to learn as much as possible about the prospective company. The Internet is an excellent tool to assist you in finding up-to-date information about a company. Annual reports and information found in journals, books, or in the library will not be as current as what you will find on the Internet. World Wide Web sites are constantly being changed and updated.

The information that you should be investigating about a prospective company includes:

- What are the company's products and services?
- Who are the company's customers?
- What is the size of the company? Has the company grown over the last five years?
- Is the company profitable?
- Has the company laid off employees?
- How do customers and competitors view the company's products and services?
- Who are the company's major competitors?
- What is the corporate culture like?
- Is the employee turnover rate low, high, or average?
- Are work schedules flexible?
- How many hours a day do employees work?
- What is the typical hiring process?
- Is the organization non-profit or for-profit? There are differences in how these types of organizations operate.

CHAPTER 11
Guided Tour...
Using the Internet for Career Exploration and Job Opportunities

• •

This chapter provides a guided tour of

- ↪ how to use the Internet for career exploration.
- ↪ how to use the Internet to find job opportunities in business.
- ↪ World Wide Web sites to explore for employment and job opportunities.
- ↪ Internet resources for finding information on companies.
- ↪ Internet Business Directories.

Job Search 1 uses Internet resources for finding a job in management training. You will also learn how to research companies with posted jobs to learn more about their corporate culture and work environment.

Job Search 2 uses different Internet resources for finding information on job opportunities for accounting.

• •

Job Search 1

Finding Employment Opportunities—Management Training

There are many excellent Internet resources for assisting you with your career exploration. This guided tour takes you on a journey to Web sites with career and business resources for employment opportunities in management training. The same resources can be used for finding other business jobs for which you are qualified.

> **NOTE**
> There are many ways to find employment opportunities and information about businesses. The more knowledgeable you are about using Internet resources for finding information, the more options you will have open to you. This example merely serves as one pathway you might take.

STEP 1
Explore job opportunities. Visit Internet's Online Career Center to search for management training jobs by keyword search.
http://www.occ.com/occ

FIGURE 11.1
Online Career Center's Home Page to find job opportunities

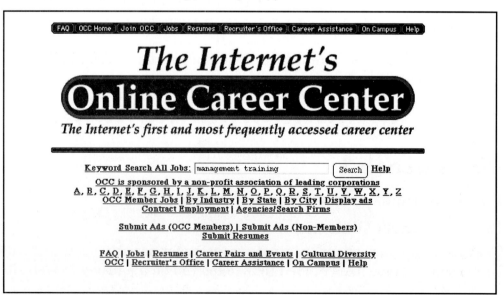

This resource has links to Frequently Asked Questions, Jobs, Résumés, Career Fairs and Events, Career Assistance, and much more. Before you begin, you may want to explore some of these links. Visit the Career Assistance Center for information on writing electronic résumés and how to submit a résumé to the Online Career Center.

STEP 2

Search for a job. Use the search tool at this site to search for management training employment opportunities. In the **Keyword Search** field, type in the job description; in this case, *management training*. Click on the **Search** button. See Figure 11.2 for the results of this search.

FIGURE 11.2

Search results from the Online Career Center using keywords, *management training*

```
14. [Jun 24] US-PA-Network Administrator- AAA Mid-Atlantic
15. [Jun 24] US-MARKETING and SALES PROFESSIONALS- RCI NATIONAL SEARCH
16. [Jun 24] US-MARKETING and SALES PROFESSIONALS- RCI NATIONAL SEARCH
17. [Jun 24] US- MARKETING and SALES PROFESSIONALS- RCI NATIONAL SEARCH
18. [Jun 24] US-MARKETING and SALES PROFESSIONALS- RCI NATIONAL SEARCH
19. [Jun 24] US-MARKETING and SALES PROFESSIONALS- RCI NATIONAL SEARCH
20. [Jun 24] US-MARKETING and SALES PROFESSIONALS- RCI NATIONAL SEARCH
21. [Jun 24] US-NY-Director of Corporate Sales - OMNIPOINT
22. [Jun 24] US-NY-Customer Service Team Leader - OMNIPOINT
23. [Jun 24] US-NY-Manager - Customer Service Training - OMNIPOINT
24. [Jun 24] US-PA-Customer Support Specialists- Delta Health Systems
```

When you click on the first link to Manager—Customer Service Training OMNIPOINT you are given this information about the job.

```
Later this year, OMNIPOINT will be the first provider of PCS
services in the greater New York area,
bringing on a new era of advanced DIGITAL WIRELESS
COMMUNICATIONS and innovative services.
We are seeking a few highly accomplished individuals, from
both inside and outside the wireless industry,
to fill out a senior management team that is already unrival
in the industry.

Develop and customize customer service, billing, P/C training
programs. Facilitate programs developed
internally and monitor their effectiveness through analysis.
```

235

STEP 3

Note companies of interest. List companies of interest from your search. You will use the Internet to research these companies to learn more about them. For example, in the search results for management training opportunities, the company OMNIPOINT may have interested you. Note their name to research them on the Internet.

STEP 4

Learn about companies where jobs are offered. There are many ways to learn more about companies. In this instance, we will use the search engine, Excite, to research Omnipoint to learn more about the company, its products, and services. The search produces a link to the Omnipoint Home Page.

FIGURE 11.3

Excite search for Omnipoint links to the company's Home Page

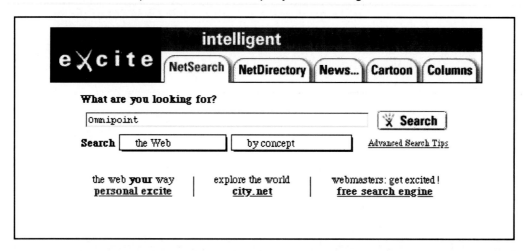

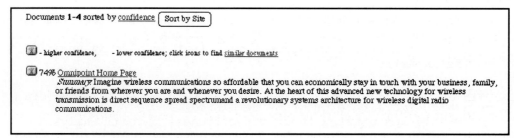

FIGURE 11.4
Omnipoint Home Page

Welcome To Our Home Page

LEARN MORE ABOUT OUR TECHNOLOGY

Imagine wireless communications so affordable that you can economically stay in touch with your business, family, or friends from wherever you are and whenever you desire. Affordable wireless communications without the interference or dropped calls often associated with conventional cellular technology. Imagine safe, secure communications and data transfer at speeds recently thought to be unobtainable.

At Omnipoint Corporation, our engineers have done more than merely imagine --- they've developed and produced systems that do all this, and more.

At the heart of this advanced new technology for wireless transmission is **direct sequence spread spectrum** and a revolutionary **systems architecture** for wireless digital radio communications. The leader in the commercial development and implementation of this technology: **Omnipoint**.

Already, the communications industry is embracing Omnipoint's revolutionary personal communications system (PCS), which has now been tested in over 30 cities accross the US. Industry leaders, including America's largest telephone and cable television companies have also joined Omnipoint in entering the 21st century of wireless communication.

Even the Federal Communications Commision has recognized the potential of Omnipoint systems, with a prestigious Pioneer's Preference award --- an award granting Omnipoint a PCS operating license for the New York Major Trading Area (MTA) and it's population base of almost 27,000,000.

The job search information indicated that Omnipoint was located in Mountain Lakes, New Jersey. You may want to research this city or town to learn more about where the company is located. In Job Search 2, you will learn how to find information on a city.

Job Search 2

Finding Employment Opportunities—Accounting

As you explore and use career and job-related Internet resources, you will find that there is no single Web site that provides all the information and tools that you will need to help you find a job.

You will find that many Web sites have a search tool to help you locate jobs and companies. Before you conduct a search, be sure you understand how the search engine can be used most effectively to find information.

Select links to **Options** or **Help** to learn more about the search tool. Other pages will provide you with information on how to conduct a search.

STEP 1

Explore jobs opportunities. Visit America's Job Bank to search for employment opportunities in accounting.
http://www.ajb.dni.us/index.html

FIGURE 11.5
Home Page for America's Job Bank

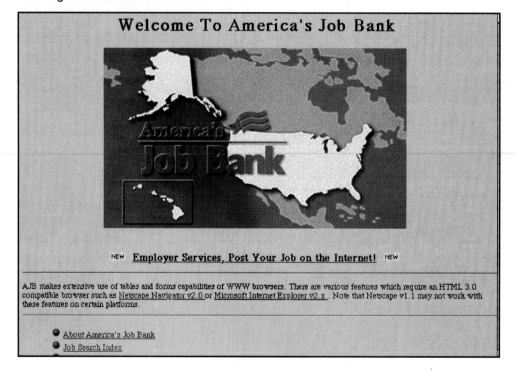

STEP 2

Select the link to the Job Search Index (shown in Fig 11.6). Select Keyword Search.

FIGURE 11.6

Clicking on the **Job Search Index** link takes you to the
Job Search Index Web page

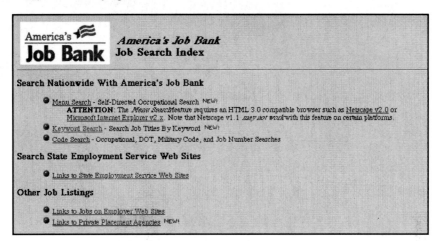

FIGURE 11.7

America's Job Bank page for finding a job by
location and job title

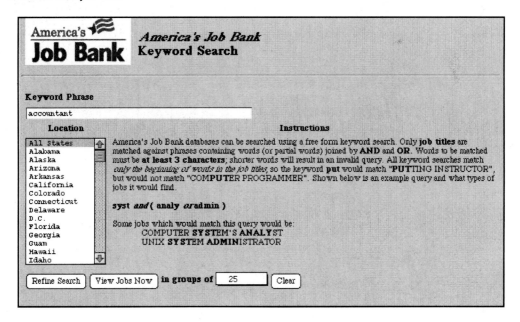

STEP 3

Select keyword search by job titles. Notice the difference in searching criteria used by the America's Job Bank in comparison to the Online Career Center.

Read the following instructions for conducting a search:

> America's Job Bank databases can be searched using a free form keyword search. Only job titles are matched against phrases containing words (or partial words) joined by AND and OR. Words to be matched must be at least 3 characters; shorter words will result in an invalid query. Listed below are examples of job titles.
>
> COMPUTER SYSTEMS ANALYST
> UNIX SYSTEM ADMINISTRATOR

FIGURE 11.8

Search produced 286 leads for jobs
under the keyword *accountant*

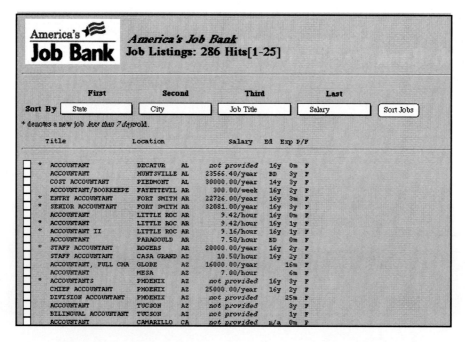

Notice that this search engine will sort jobs in an order that you select: city, state, job title, or salary. For this search, jobs were sorted first by state, then city.

To learn about each job, click once in the box next to each of the job postings you are interested in reading about. Then click on the button, **View Jobs**.

FIGURE 11.9

Job description for an accountant in San Francisco, California

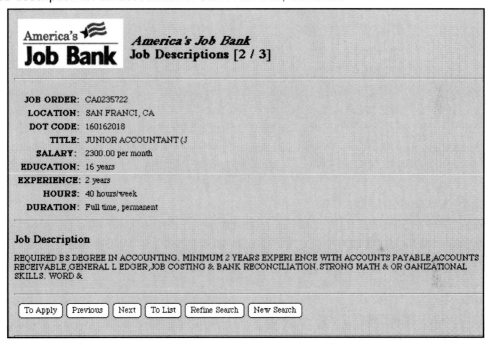

Click on the **Next** button for a job description of the second job you are interested in.

At the bottom of each page is a button to apply for the job if you feel you are interested and qualify. By selecting this option, you may learn more about the company or the recruiter posting the job.

FIGURE 11.10

Example of online application form for a job

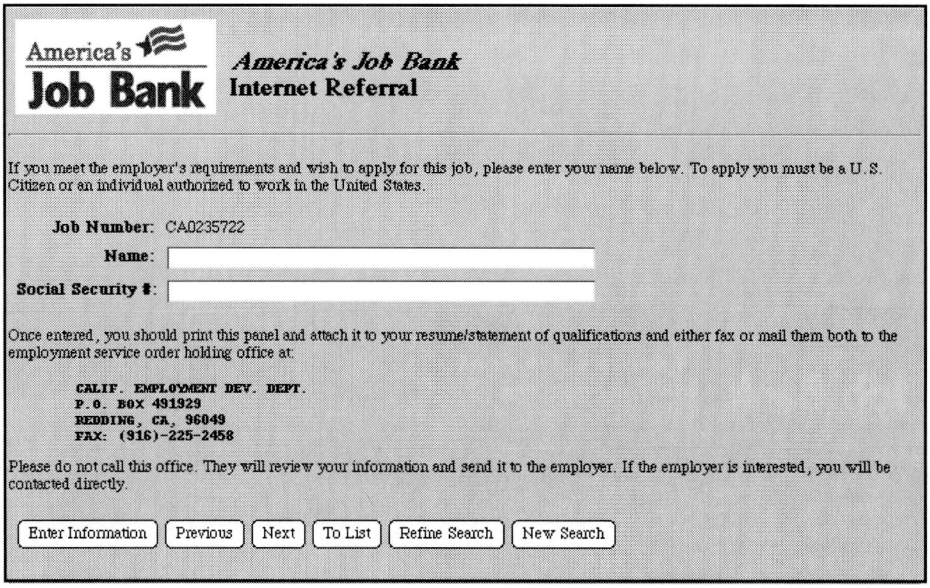

STEP 4

Learn more about the cities where these jobs are located. After reading the job description you may be interested in applying for the job, but would first like to learn more about the city where the job is located.

To learn about the cities for the jobs you selected, visit City.Net. **http://www.city.net**

This Web site (Fig. 11.11) provides options for learning about cities by visiting their Most Popular U.S. City Destinations or by conducting a keyword search.

Several of the accounting jobs were located in San Francisco, California. Select the link to San Francisco under Most Popular U.S. Cities (Fig. 11.12) or click on the search button and enter **San Francisco, California.**

FIGURE 11.11

Web site for City.Net

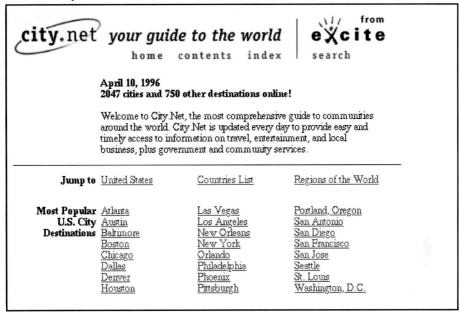

FIGURE 11.12

City.Net's links to San Francisco information

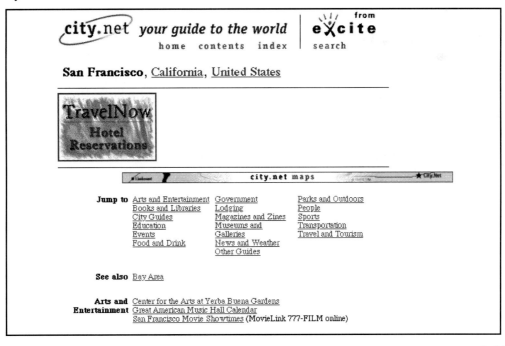

STEP 5

Use other career and job resources to search for jobs. Two other excellent Internet sites to visit to assist in finding jobs are Career Web and the Monster Board. Their job searches differ from Online Career Center and America's Job Bank. Enter in this URL for Career Web. **http://www.cweb.com**

FIGURE 11.13
Career Web's search tool for finding a job by discipline and state/country

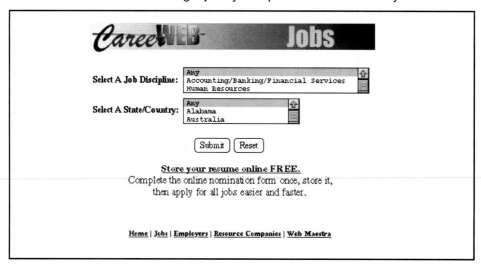

Notice that this job site asks you to select a job discipline and a state or country of your preference. Scroll down through the job disciplines to find one that best matches the job you are searching for. For your first search you may want to select Any State/Country to see what is available. Later you can refine your search.

STEP 6

Visit the Monster Board to investigate its job search resources. **http://www.monster.com** is its URL. When you connect to Monster Board, sign in as a first-time visitor. There is no charge for using and visiting this site.

After clicking on the two links, job opportunities and career search, you are at the page shown in Figure 11.14.

This job site presents job locations and job disciplines for you to select. For more information on each job discipline, click on the link for more information. After you select a location and discipline and conduct a search, you may be asked to refine your search.

> **NOTE**
>
> After using four different Internet Job resources, you now have some knowledge about Internet tools for finding job opportunities. You should also have a better understanding of how these resources differ in helping you to find a job. As with all Internet resources, you will need to use many different tools to help you find the information you are searching for. You will find that some tools are more helpful than others for specific types of information requested.

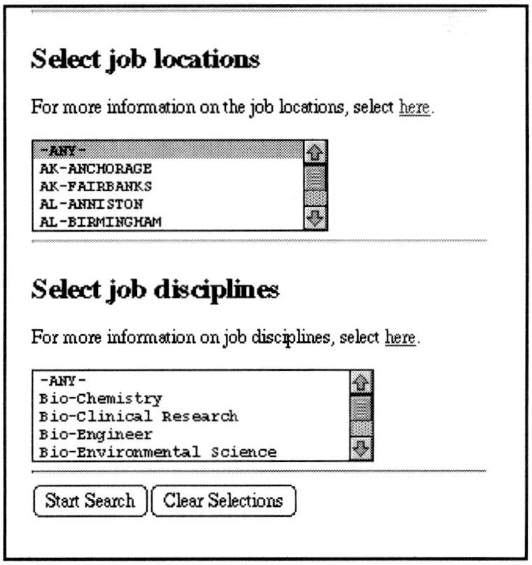

FIGURE 11.14
Monster Board's search options using location and job discipline criteria

Select job locations

For more information on the job locations, select here.

| -ANY- |
| AK-ANCHORAGE |
| AK-FAIRBANKS |
| AL-ANNISTON |
| AL-BIRMINGHAM |

Select job disciplines

For more information on job disciplines, select here.

| -ANY- |
| Bio-Chemistry |
| Bio-Clinical Research |
| Bio-Engineer |
| Bio-Environmental Science |

[Start Search] [Clear Selections]

Monster Board also has options for keyword searches.

Internet Resources to Explore

Employment and Job Opportunities

Refer to pages 224-226 for the best Internet resources to explore to help you find career and job opportunities.

Internet Business Directories

Internet Business Directories are resources to find information on a company.

Apollo

This Web site provides options for searching for a company by country and keyword. **http://apollo.co.uk**

Linkstar

Linkstar provides keyword search options, plus a listing of categories for finding information. **http://www.linkstar.com**

New Rider's WWW Yellow Pages

New Rider's World Wide Web Yellow Pages offers business search options by keyword or by category. A keyword search for jobs produces numerous job-related links. **http://www.mcp.com/newriders/wwwyp**

Nynex Interactive Yellow Pages

The largest of the business directories has options for searching for companies by business location, category, or business name. **http://www.niyp.com**

Virtual Yellow Pages

The Virtual Yellow Pages is a comprehensive and easy-to-use directory of Web sites and information. **http://www.vyp.com**

World Wide Yellow Pages

World Wide Yellow Pages has a link to assist you with finding information on businesses. **http://www.yellow.com**

GLOSSARY

applets: Mini-applications that a software program such as Netscape downloads and executes.

ASCII (text) files: One of the file transfer modes (binary is another mode) used when transferring files on the Internet. ASCII treats the file as a set of characters that can be read by the com puter receiving the ASCII text. ASCII does not recognize text formatting such as boldface, underline, tab stops, or fonts.

binary file: Another transfer mode available for transferring Internet files. In the binary mode, files are transferred which are identical in appearance to the original document.

Binhex (BINary HEXadecimal): A method for converting non-text files (non-ASCII) into ASCII. Used in e-mail programs that can handle only ASCII.

Bit: A single-digit number, either a 1 or a zero, that represents the smallest unit of computerized data.

bookmarks: A feature providing the user with the opportunity to mark favorite pages for fast and easy access. Netscape's bookmarks can be organized hierarchically and customized by the user through the Bookmark List dialog box.

boolean operators: Phrases or words such as "and," "or," and "not" that limit a search using Internet search engines.

browser: A client program that interprets and displays HTML documents.

client: A software program assisting in contacting a server somewhere on the Net for information. Examples of client software programs are

Gopher, Netscape, Veronica, and Archie. An Archie client runs on a system configured to contact a specific Archie database to query for information.

compression: A process by which a file or a folder is made smaller. The three primary purposes of compression are to save disk space, to save space when doing a backup, and to speed the transmission of a file when transferring by way of a modem or network.

domain name: The unique name that identifies an Internet site. Names have two or more parts separated by a dot such as **xplora.com**

finger: An Internet software tool for locating people on the Internet. The most common use is to see if an individual has an account at a particular Internet site.

fire wall: A combination of hardware and software that separates a local area network into two parts for security purposes.

frames: A new feature of Netscape Navigator makes it possible to create multiple windows on a Netscape page. This is an example of a Web page divided into several windows called *frames*. To navigate within frames and to save bookmarks you will use your mouse. To move forward and back within frames, position your cursor within the frame and hold down the mouse button (Macintosh users); Windows users hold down the right mouse button. A pop-up menu appears.

Choose **Back in Frame** or **Forward in Frame**. To bookmark a frame, place your cursor over the link to the frame and hold down the mouse button. A different pop-up menu appears. Select **Add Bookmark for this Link**. To print a frame, click the desired frame and select **Print Frame** from the **File** menu.from the **File** menu.

FTP (File Transfer Protocol): Protocol for transferring files between computers on the Internet.

GIF (Graphic Interface Format): A format developed by CompuServe, Inc. for storing complex graphics. This format is one of two used for storing graphics in HTML documents.

Helper Applications: Programs used by Netscape to read files retrieved from the Internet. Different server protocols are used by Netscape to transfer files: HTTP, NNTP, SMTP, and FTP. Each protocol supports different file formats for text, images, video, and sound. When these files are received by Netscape, the external helper applications read, interpret, and display the file.

History List: Netscape keeps track of your Internet journeys. Sites that you visit are listed in the History List found under the **Go** pull-down menu. Click on an Internet site on your list, and you will be linked to that destination.

Home Page: The starting point for World Wide Web exploration. The Home Page contains highlighted words and icons that link to text, graphic, video, and sound files. Home Pages can be developed by anyone: Internet Providers, universities, businesses, and individuals. Netscape allows you to select which Home Page is displayed when you launch the program.

HTML (HyperText Markup Language): A programming language used to create a Web page. This includes the text of the document, its structure, and links to other documents. HTML also includes the programming for accessing and displaying media such as images, video, and sound.

HTTP (HyperText Transfer Protocol): One protocol used by the World Wide Web to transfer information. Web documents begin with **http://**

IP address: Every computer on the Internet has a unique IP address. This number consists of four parts separated by dots such as 198.68.32.1

JavaScript: A new programming language developed by Sun Microsystems that makes it possible to incorporate mini-applications called *applets* onto a Web page.

JPEG (Joint Photographic Experts Group): A file format for graphics (photographs, complex images, and video stills) that uses compression.

live objects: Java brings life and interaction to Web pages by making it possible to create live objects. Move your mouse over an image of a house and see the lights go on. Move your mouse to a picture of a woman and hear her welcome you to her Home Page.

MIME (Multimedia Internet Mail Extension): Most multimedia files on the Internet are MIME. The MIME type refers to the type of file: text, HTML, images, video, or sound. When a browser such as Netscape retrieves a file from a server, the server provides the MIME type to establish whether the file format can be read by the software's built-in capabilities or, if not, whether a suitable helper application is available to read the file.

newsgroups: Large distributed bulletin board systems that consist of several thousand specialized discussion groups. Messages are posted to a bulletin board by e-mail for others to read.

NNTP (News Server): A server protocol used by Netscape for transferring Usenet news. Before you can read Usenet news, you must enter the name of your news server to interact with Usenet newsgroups. The news server name is entered in the Mail and News dialog box (**Options** pull-down menu; **Preferences**; Mail and News).

page: A file or document in Netscape that contains hypertext links to multimedia resources.

platform: Netscape Navigator 2.0 and 3.0 are referred to as a platform rather than a browser. A platform program makes it possible for developers to build applications onto it.

PPP (Point-to-Point Protocol): A method by which a computer may use a high-speed modem and a standard telephone line to have full Internet access. A PPP or SLIP connection is required to use graphical interfaces with the Internet such as Netscape Navigator and Explorer. Using a PPP or SLIP connection enables you to point and click your way around the Internet.

.sea (self-extracting archives): A file name extension indicating a compression method used by Macintosh computers. Files whose names end in .sea are compressed archives that can be decompressed by double-clicking on the program icon.

search engine: Software programs designed for seeking information on the Internet. Some of these programs search by keyword within a document, title, index, or directory.

server: A computer running software that allows another computer (a client) to communicate with it for information exchange.

shell account: The most basic type of Internet connection. A shell account allows you to dial into the Internet at your provider's site. Your Internet software is run on the computer at that site. On a shell account your Internet interface is text-based. There are no pull-down menus, icons, or graphics. Some Internet providers offer a menu system of Internet options; others merely provide a Unix system prompt, usually a percent sign or a dollar sign. You must know the commands to enter at the prompt to access the Internet.

SLIP (Serial Line Internet Protocol): A method by which a computer with a high speed modem may connect directly to the Internet through a standard telephone line. A SLIP account is needed to use Netscape. SLIP is currently being replaced with PPP (Point-to-Point Protocol).

SMTP (Simple Mail Transport Protocol): A protocol used by the Internet for electronic mail. Before using Netscape e-mail, the host name of the Internet provider's mail server must be designated. The mail server name is entered in the Mail and News dialog box (**Options** pull-down menu; **Preferences**; Mail and News).

source file: When saved as "source," the document is preserved with its embedded HTML instructions that format the Internet page.

TCP/IP (Transmission Control Protocol/Internet Protocol): The protocol upon which the Internet is based and which supports transmission of data.

toolbar: Navigational buttons used in graphical interface applications.

URL (Uniform Resource Locator): URLs are a standard for locating Internet documents. They use an addressing system for other Internet protocols such as access to Gopher menus, FTP file retrieval, and Usenet newsgroups. The format for a URL is **protocol://server-name:/path**

URL object: Any resource accessible on the World Wide Web: text documents, sound files, movies, and images.

Usenet: Developed in the 1970s for communication among computers at various universities. In the early 1980s, Usenet was being used for electronic discussions on a wide variety of topics and soon became a tool for communication. Today, Usenet groups are analogous to a cafe where people from everywhere in the world gather to discuss and share ideas on topics of common interest.

viewer: Programs needed to display graphics, sound, and video. For example, pictures stored as a GIF image have the file name extension ".gif" and need a gif helper application to display the image. Netscape has the required viewers (external helper applications) built into the software. A list of programs required to view files can be found in the Helper Application menu of Netscape. Open the **Options** pull-down menu, select **Preferences**, then **Helper Applications**.

VRML (Virtual Reality Modeling Language): a programming language that makes 3-dimensional virtual reality experiences possible on Web pages.

REFERENCES

Angell, D. (1996, March). The ins and outs of ISDN. *Internet World*, 78-82.

Bennahum, D. S. (1995, May). Domain street, U.S.A. *NetGuide*, 51-56.

Butler, M. (1994). *How to Use the Internet*. Emeryville, CA: Ziff-Davis Press.

Career Center (1996). [Online]. Available: http://www.monster.com/home.html
or http://199.94.216.77:80/jobseek/center/cclinks.htm

CareerMosaic Career Resource Center (1996). [Online]. Available:
http://www.careermosaic.com/cm/crc/

Conte, R. (1996, May). Guiding lights. *Internet World*, 41-44.

Dixon, P. (1995, May). Jobs on the web. *SKY*, 130-138.

Ellsworth, J. H., & Ellsworth, M.V. (1994). *The Internet Business Book*. New York:
John Wiley & Sons, Inc.

Grusky, S. (1996, February). Winning résumés. *Internet World*, 58-68.

Leibs, S. (1995, June). Doing business on the net. *NetGuide*, 48-53.

Leshin, C. (1996). *Internet Adventures—Step-by-Step Guide to Finding and Using
Educational Resources*. Boston: Allyn and Bacon.

Leshin, C. (1997). *Netscape Adventures—Step-by-Step Guide to Netscape Navigator
and the World Wide Web*. Upper Saddle River, NJ: Prentice Hall.

Miller, D. (1994, October). The many faces of the Internet. *Internet World*, 34-38.

Netscape Communication Corporation. (1996, January/February). *Netscape
Handbook*. [Online]. Currently available by calling 1-415-528-2555 or online by
selecting the Handbook button from within Netscape.

O'Connell, G. M. (1995, May). A new pitch: Advertising on the World Wide Web is a
whole new ball game. *Internet World*, 54-56.

Reichard, K., & King, N. (1996, June). The Internet phone craze. *NetGuide*, 52-58.

Resnick, R., & Taylor, D. (1994). *The Internet Business*. Indianapolis, IN: Sams Publishing.

Richard, E. (1995, April). Anatomy of the World Wide Web. *Internet World*, 28-30.

Riley, Margaret F. (1996). Employement Opportunities and Job Resources on the Internet [Online]. Available: http://www.jobtrak.com./jobguide/

Sachs, D., & Stair, H. (1996). *Hands-on Netscape, a Tutorial for Windows users*. Upper Saddle River, NJ: Prentice Hall.

Sanchez, R. (1994, November/December). Usenet culture. *Internet World*, 38-41.

Schwartz, E. I. (1996, February). Advertising webonomics 101. *Wired*, 74-82.

Signell, K. (1995, March). Upping the ante: The ins and outs of slip/ppp. *Internet World*, 58-60.

Strangelove, M. (1995, May). The walls come down. *Internet World*, 40-44.

Taylor, D. (1994, November/December). Usenet: Past, present, future. *Internet World*, 27-30.

Vendito, G. (1996, March). Online services—how does their net access stack-up? *Internet World*, 55-65

Venditto, G. (1996, May). Search engine showdown. *Internet World*, 79-86.

Vendito, G. (1996, June). Internet phones—the future is calling. *Internet World*, 40-52.

Weiss, A. (1994, December). Gabfest—Internet relay chat. *Internet World*, 58-62.

Welz, G. (1995, May). A tour of ads online. *Internet World*, 48-50.

Wiggins, R. W. (1994, March). Files come in flavors. *Internet World*, 52-56.

Wiggins, R. W. (1994, April). Webolution: The evolution of the revolutionary World Wide Web. *Internet World*, 33-38.

Wilson, S. (1995). *World Wide Web Design Guide*. Indianapolis, IN: Hayden Books.

APPENDIX I
Connecting to the Internet

Connecting to the Internet

There are three ways to connect to the Internet:

- a network
- an online service
- a SLIP/PPP connection

Network Connection

Network connections are most often found in colleges, schools, businesses, or government agencies and use dedicated lines to provide fast access to all Internet resources. Special hardware such as routers may be required at the local site. Prices depend on bandwidth and the speed of the connection.

Online Services

Examples of online services include America Online, CompuServe, Prodigy, Delphi, and Microsoft Network. Online services are virtual communities that provide services to their subscribers including electronic mail, discussion forums on topics of interest, real time chats, business and advertising opportunities, software libraries, stock quotes, online newspapers, and Internet resources (Gopher, FTP, newsgroups). There are advantages and disadvantages to these online services.

Advantages

The advantages to online services include:

- easy to install and use,
- content offered by provider,
- easy to find and download software,
- easy-to-use e-mail, and
- virtual community of resources and people.

Commercial online services are excellent places to begin exploring and learning about the use of e-mail and accessing network information and resources.

Disadvantages

The disadvantages to online services include:

- expensive to use,
- do not always access all Internet resources such as Gopher, FTP, and Telnet, and
- must use the online service's e-mail program and Internet browser.

Online services charge an average of $9.95 per month for 5 hours of online time. Additional online time is billed at rates of $2.95 to $5.95 per hour. Some services charge more for being online at peak hours such as during the day.

In comparison, an Internet access provider may charge $15-$30 per month for 100-to-unlimited hours of online time. Prices vary depending on your locality and the Internet access provider.

SLIP/PPP Connection

Internet access providers offer SLIP (Serial Line Interface Protocol) or PPP (Point-to-Point Protocol) connections (SLIP/PPP). This service is referred to as *Dial-Up-Networking* and makes it possible for your PC to dial into their server and communicate with other computers on the Internet. Once you have established a PPP, SLIP, or direct Internet connection, you can use any software that speaks the Internet language called TCP/IP. There are several TCP/IP software applications including Eudora, Netscape Navigator, and Explorer.

Internet service providers should give you the required TCP/IP software to get you connected to the Internet. Additionally, many will provide Internet applications such as Eudora, Netscape Navigator, and Explorer. Prices are usually based on hours of usage, bandwidth, and locality.

TCP/IP and SLIP/PPP Software

Macintosh Software

TCP/IP software for the Macintosh is called MacTCP and is supplied by Apple. Two popular software choices necessary to implement either SLIP or PPP are MacPPP or MacSLIP. Using one of these programs with MacTCP creates a direct Internet connection.

Your Internet access provider should give you software that has already been configured for connecting your Mac to the Internet.

Commercial Online Services

America Online
http://www.aol.com
(800) 827-6347
e-mail: postmaster@aol.com

AT&T WorldNet Services
http://www.att.com
(800) 831-5269
e-mail: webmaster@att.com

CompuServe
(800) 848-8990
e-mail: 70006,101@compuserve.com

Microsoft Network
http://www.msn.com
(800) 426-9400

Prodigy
(800) 776-3449

The WELL
http://www.well.com
(415) 332-4335
e-mail: web-info@well.com

APPENDIX II
Finding an Internet Provider

• •

There are several Web sites to help you find an Internet access provider.
http://thelist.com
http://www.clari.net/iap/iapcode.htm
http://www.primus.com/providers

To find the names of providers in your area, click on the link to your area code. You will find descriptive information of providers in your area code and a description of their services.

> **NOTE**
>
> All providers that service your area will be found by the area code listing.

Tips For Finding a Provider

If your area code is not listed
There are providers who have nationwide access. Some of the Web sites have information on these service providers.

If there is no local dial-in number
Look for service providers that are the closest to you or who have an 800 - number dial-in access. Many providers are also listed on these Web sites.

Choosing a provider
Contact providers by phone, fax, or electronic mail. If you want to use Netscape or Explorer you will need to get a SLIP or a PPP account.

Ask about the following:

- Type of Internet accounts available.

- Price and hours of access. How much will it cost per month for a SLIP or PPP account? How many hours of Internet access are included? An average price is $20 per month for 150 hours of graphical access.

- Technical support. Does the provider offer technical support? What are the hours (days, nights, weekends, holidays)? Is support free?

- Software. Do they provide the TCP/IP software? Is the software custom configured? Do they provide free copies of an e-mail program such as Eudora or a Web browser such as Netscape Navigator or Explorer? Good Internet providers will provide custom configured TCP/IP software and the essential Internet navigation and communication software.

> **NOTE**
> If you are using Windows 95 you will need to get information for configuring your Windows 95 TCP/IP software. At the time of this printing you cannot get TCP/IP software custom configured for Windows 95.

APPENDIX III
Using an Internet Navigational Suite

● ●

Internet front-end navigational suites are complete packages of tools that make it easier for you to connect to the Internet. In the past these suites provided separate software applications packaged together. The newer versions offer integrated software programs that are simple and save time. Every aspect of the Internet is easier, including your initial Internet set-up, Internet navigation, and downloading files using the File Transfer Protocol (FTP).

All of the front-end packages include the following:

- a configuration utility for establishing your Internet service
- e-mail software
- a graphical Web browser
- a newsgroup reader
- an FTP utility

The configuration utility assists you with dialing up a service provider and opening an account. The service providers listed in the software are usually limited to several large companies.

NOTE

- The cost for an Internet connection provided by the companies listed in front-end suites may be more expensive than the cost of using a local Internet provider.

- Integrated software packages may not allow you to use other e-mail programs or Web browsers.

Suggested Internet Navigational Suites

- EXPLORE Internet: (800) 863-4548
- IBM Internet Connection For Windows: (800) 354-3222
- Internet Anywhere: (519) 888-9910
- Internet Chameleon: (408) 973-7171
- Internet In A Box: (800) 557-9614 or (800) 777-9638
- Netscape Navigator Personal Edition: (415) 528-2555
- SuperHighway Access: (800) 929-3054

INDEX